debbietravis' paintedhouse

kids' rooms

debbietravis' paintedhouse
kids' rooms

more than 80 innovative projects from cradle to college

Debbie Travis with Barbara Dingle

Photographs by George Ross

Clarkson Potter / Publishers
New York

Published by Clarkson Potter/Publishers,
New York, New York. Member of the
Crown Publishing Group, a division of
Random House, Inc.
www.randomhouse.com

CLARKSON N. POTTER is a trademark and
POTTER and colophon are registered
trademarks of Random House, Inc.

Printed in Japan

Design by Jan Derevjanik

Library of Congress Cataloging-in-
Publication Data
Travis, Debbie.
Debbie Travis' painted house kids' rooms/by
Debbie Travis.
1. House painting—Amateurs' manuals.
2. Interior decoration—Amateurs' manuals.
3. Children's rooms. I. Title: Painted
house kids' rooms. II. Title.

TT323.T69   2002
745.5—dc21   2001054566

ISBN 0-609-80551-7

10 9 8 7 6 5 4

This book is dedicated to the Travis clan of children: my glorious two boys, Josh and Max, and all their American and British cousins, Daniel and Nathan, Ben, Henry and Freddie, and Amelia and Beatrice.

acknowledgments

Just as the playground is packed with clusters of children using their vivid imaginations, so is the production of a book. It is a major team effort of creative people working together to write, design, and photograph each page. Although it's a huge amount of work, the hours are always filled with fun and laughter. The talented Clarkson Potter group is made up of Marysarah Quinn, Jan Derevjanik, Jean Lynch, and Joan Denman. The leader of the publishing team is Margot Schupf, my editor, who keeps us all going with gentle prods.

Barbara Dingle works in her corner of the playground madly writing, while George Ross photographs the rooms with the enthusiasm of a preschooler, and Ernst Hellrung photographs all the step-by-steps. Thanks also to Christopher Dew and Robert Pelletier.

Dana MacKimmie is the fastest runner, so her job is to oversee the step-by-steps, keep track of all the photography, and chase everyone with their deadlines.

You need a youthful personality to design children's rooms, and the Painted House team have tireless spirit. I would very much like to thank my art directors, Alison Osborne and Anne Côté, and their gang of artists and painters. This incredible team consists of James Simon, Susan Pistawka, Lynn Roulston, Stephanie Robertson, Lynne Charest, Pauline St.-Amand, Yves Prud'homme, Mr. "K" Koffkinsky, Deborah Goldsmith, Sharon Harwood, Donna White, Linda Buckingham, Ann Francis Oakes, Jill Hannerford and Heather Gilmour. Interior designers Valorie Finnie and Elaine Miller shop for and dress each room with a winning combination of childlike abandon and impeccable taste.

Finally, I would like to thank all the children who have appeared on *The Painted House* television series, and allowed us into their bedrooms and playrooms.

contents

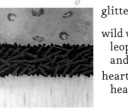

preface

Like all women, I wear many hats, and the most important one of all is being a mom. I have two sons who are absolutely typical of their gender and age. Life for them revolves around games, sports, the telephone, e-mail, movies, television, and, when they can fit it in, schoolwork. Decorating does not register on their agenda, but it is an important part of their lives even if they don't know it. There is no other room in the house than a child's that incorporates such essential elements—comfort, practicality, safety, and, of course, fun.

It is a joy to decorate a child's room, because unlike the rest of the home, there is no one else to consider. Children know their likes and dislikes and their favorite colors, and they have no problem using their imagination. If I were to ask a group of five-year-olds to pick a color for their bedroom walls, I can be sure that not one would choose beige, taupe, or mushroom. As we mature we become more conservative in our tastes, either through fear of making a mistake or desire to solve the dilemma of creating a surrounding that pleases not only ourselves but also our family and friends.

During the many years of filming my television series, *The Painted House*, the most exciting shows have invariably been the ones working with children. We have always involved the kids right from the early development and design of their rooms, and it is their input that inspires us to create successful makeovers. When you work on your own children's rooms, whatever the age, listen to their ideas and let your imagination soar along with theirs. You will fulfill not only your children's dreams and fantasies but yours as well.

introduction

Decorating children's rooms is an ongoing affair—the planning
begins before they are even born and evolves and changes until
they tower over you. Whether your little ones are starting to read
or starting to streak their hair, their rooms should be as individual
as they are. Children's rooms should provide a practical and comfortable environment, but they must also be a stimulating place
for both creative play and learning.

This book includes a host of ideas for painting and decorating children's bedrooms and playrooms. It takes you from the cradle days up to the time they leave for college, and we've also included a section filled with rainy day projects. Some of these projects your children can do themselves, and many you'll want to do along with their helping hands. If you are a beginner, read Start Right (pages 14–27) to familiarize yourself with the necessary preparation and product information. This will ensure a safe and professional finish for your chosen projects.

Designing rooms for children requires slightly different planning than designing other rooms in the home. Throughout *Kids' Rooms* we have combined the essential elements to be taken into consideration while you think about the arrangement of colors, fabrics, and furnishings. Your children spend a great proportion of their lives playing, working, and sleeping in these rooms. Making them healthy, practical, and welcoming is time well spent.

a safe place

Whether you are planning a nursery or a teenager's room, safety is crucial. Fabrics and furnishings must be checked carefully along with their installation. The government sets out safety standards that must be met for children's products. In the nursery make sure that the baby's bed, usually a crib, meets these standards. The crib bars must be close together so that a baby's head cannot slip through. All paint, varnish, or other surface finishes must be nontoxic. With new furniture this is usually not a problem, but if you are using secondhand pieces it's important to check what type of paint has been used. Window blinds should have a single cord, not a loop cord, for moving the blind up and down, and be sure to position the crib away from the window, radiators, or any shelving a toddler could stand, climb, or pull on. In addition, be sure that toy boxes, trunks, and chests are free of locks or clasps and that the tops or lids are light enough that even a small toddler can push it open from the inside.

Electrical cords can be a hazard at any age. Tape them to the floor or run them behind furniture, and buy childproof safety plugs for the electrical sockets. Once electrical equipment such as a computer or sound system enters the scene, use a power strip—a multiplug strip with its own switch.

Any beds, chairs, tables, and ladders will be climbed on and knocked about, so this furniture must be well made, solid, and practical.

Bolt bookshelves or other furniture that may topple over to the wall or floor. Good storage solutions will help keep the rooms free of scattered toys and clothing and safer and more enjoyable to play in. Children are explorers, and it's your job to make their expeditions as safe as possible.

allergies

Unfortunately, allergies have become a part of many children's lives. Today there is an increasing number of products and materials that can be used in children's rooms to alleviate their discomfort. The cork floor (page 46) is an example of a nonallergenic, practical, and good-looking alternative to carpets. For most allergy sufferers, there are down duvets and comforters that are available as well as mattress and pillow covers that seal out molds, mildew, and dust mites that live in bedding.

Toxic cleaning agents, dyes, and oil-based paints now have environmentally friendly alternatives that make decorating safe and more enjoyable. Even the mild fumes from water-based paint may affect an asthmatic when it is first applied, but the fast drying time generally means the child can return to his or her room quickly. Look in the Resources for an informative web site on healthy rooms and products.

plan along with your child

The planning stage can be the most fun of all. Children's input is imperative for a successful room so that you can understand the room from their perspective at the start. One of my son's friends now refuses to sleep in his bedroom after his mother decorated his room in a dark tartan plaid while he was at camp. The room looks fabulous, but the boy was not consulted and disliked the dark colors.

To avoid this frustration, take the surprise out of the scenario and work together. What are your children's hobbies, dreams, favorite personalities, and colors? What makes them go "Wow!"? What activities take place in the room, and how can you separate work space from play space from sleep space?

Children can understand the need for a budget at quite a young age, so don't be afraid or embarrassed to discuss less-expensive ways to accomplish the look they are dreaming about. Paint and a vivid imagination will always be your best friends when it comes to decorating on a shoestring.

Encourage your children to take part in the actual redecorating, even if it's just a small job. Older children can wield a paint roller and make personalized accessories right along with you.

rooms that grow

The practical side of your decorating decisions is the final element to consider. Flexible decorating and adaptable furnishings help you plan for the future as your children's tastes and needs change. Sturdy wooden furniture can be updated quickly with paint to keep pace (see the dressers on page 143). Storage solutions take on a sense of humor in the hope that clutter will disappear (see Storage under Wraps, page 145).

The transformations in *Kids' Rooms* are miraculous because you get maximum impact using materials such as paint, fabric, paper, wood trim, and moldings that are easily changed. It will take only a weekend to revise a gentle nursery painted in neutrals with teddy bear paws for baby (page 40) to a teenager's wild palette of grass green with fuchsia feather borders (pages 60–67).

Move furniture around and reinvent what you have by changing hardware, adding a new top, or building in storage. Then go to town on a few accessories that kick up the theme. The CD Picture Frame (page 156) is a clever way to show off favorite photographs. Decorate a lampshade or create an entire wall for messages, study lists, and memos. Practical never has to mean dull.

Dream up some fascinating living spaces with and for your children. And then, before you begin the job, read Start Right (pages 14–27) on decorating basics, just to make sure your work lasts until the next stage rolls around.

start right
paint basics

If you have never tackled a paint project before, then you are in
for a treat. Applying a coat of paint or a paint technique will
transform any room instantly. It's magical! There is some work
involved, to be sure, but the "wow" factor will more than make it
worthwhile. Paints, rollers, and brushes are not expensive, and
are available at your closest hardware or paint store. Each product
is labeled to take the confusion out of the vast assortment, and

the sales staff are generally knowledgeable and helpful. Let them know that you are a beginner and they will steer you in the right direction.

I use water-based paints and glazes for all the projects in this book as they are more environmentally friendly, almost odorless, and dry quickly, and the brushes, rollers, and paint trays are easily cleaned with soap and water. They are also safest to use with or around children. Where exceptions are made, such as with the epoxy finish on the Icy Desktop on page 100 or the spray varnish for My Magnets on page 162, I have made a note on the project to move children out of the room while the work is going on. The chart on page 16 indicates which materials and tools in this book are safe for children to use on their own, are best used alongside a parent, or are exclusively for adult use. Throughout the book you will also see notes that offer project safety tips or quick tips.

Always read each project's materials and tools list and step-by-step instructions carefully before you start. If you use products other than the ones we list, be sure to read the label on use and safety for that product.

note to mom or dad

However fabulous your child's design or color choice for his or her room is, it's important that you prepare the surfaces carefully first.

work safely

When painting a room, take the time to create a safe working environment. Clear out as much furniture as possible and cover the remaining pieces and the floor with painters' drop cloths. These are a good investment because paint leaks through newspapers and plastic sheets are slippery.

Use a stable ladder and clear enough space around the perimeter of the room to set up and move the ladder safely and easily. Extension poles will help you reach the ceiling and tops of walls, but you will need a ladder to tape off and paint clean edges (see Applying a Base Coat, page 22). Keep small children and animals at a safe distance to avoid accidents, bumps, and spills, especially when you are up on the ladder.

Wear a face mask and goggles when sanding to protect your lungs and eyes from airborne particles. When working with toxic fumes, rent or buy a mask that fits tightly over your nose and mouth and uses replaceable charcoal filters. Toxic fumes can have a faster and more serious effect on a child than on an adult.

When working on smaller projects, set aside a work space that is big enough to support the piece that you are working on plus the tools and materials you need.

It's great fun to involve young children in making something for their room, even if it's on a minor level, but never leave them unattended with pots of paint or glue and scissors. Practice the same safety procedures yourself as you do with them so that they will learn by example.

Older children may want to work on their own, but read the instructions with them first and discuss how they are going to go about the work. Make sure that any warnings and safety precautions are understood and followed.

note to mom or dad

Be aware that toxic fumes from chemical strippers, oil and metallic paints, and paint thinners can have a faster and more serious effect on a child than on an adult.

safety guidelines chart

When working with children, always take special care that you are familiar with the products, tools, and procedures followed for completing a project. This chart is only a guideline.

MATERIAL OR TOOL	PARENTS AND CHILDREN WORKING TOGETHER	PARENTS ONLY	SAFE FOR CHILDREN 9 YEARS AND OVER
Water-based paint and glaze	X		
Oil-based paint has toxic fumes and requires paint thinner for cleanup.		X	
Some metallic and pearlescent paints are toxic. Check bottle.	X	X	
All varnishes		X	
Epoxy varnish		X	
All spray paints		X	
Spray adhesives		X	
Hot-glue gun		X	
White craft glue, glue sticks	X		X
Wallpaper paste	X		
Contact cement		X	
Con-Tact paper	X		X
Safety scissors	X		X
Paintbrushes, sponges	X		X
X-acto knife		X	
Jigsaw		X	
Staple gun		X	
Indelible markers	X		
Sandpaper: sanding creates airborne dust that can be harmful. Always wear a mask.		X	

materials and tools

paints

There are basically two types of paint found at your neighborhood paint or hardware store: oil based and water based. Oil paint is known as alkyd, and water-based paint is called latex. You will also see cans of acrylic paints, which are also water based but have a different formulation from latex; these two should not be mixed together.

All the rooms in this book are decorated using latex paint because it has a low odor, is safe to use around children, and can be cleaned up with soap and water. For people who are allergic to latex paint, there are natural paints made from organic matter (see Resources, page 174), although the color selection is somewhat limited. Whatever type of paint you use, you should work in a well-ventilated room.

For smaller projects there is no need to purchase the large quantities of paint contained in most commercial cans. This is where the craft and art supply stores become invaluable. Craft paints, stencil paints, and artist's oils and acrylics are available in small quantities in numerous colors. Note that children's watercolor paints are not recommended for decorating projects as the colors are not permanent.

primers

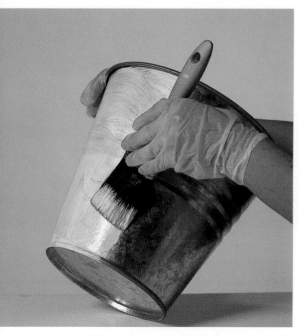

A primer is a specially formulated white paint that is applied before the base coat goes on. Primers are very important for a successful project and will always save time and money in the end. There are several different primers on the market designed for different jobs. Standard primer is used to seal plaster walls and cracks that have been filled with plaster. If you paint a base coat over raw plaster, the base coat will sink into the porous surface.

There are primers that will seal in stains like marker, lipstick, water marks, or tobacco-stained ceilings. There are also metal primers to stop metal objects from rusting once painted. Floorcloths need to be primed to seal the canvas and to give weight to the fabric so that it will lie flat on the floor.

This metal wastebasket is being primed to give it tooth for paint.

Both water- and oil-based primers are readily available. If you are painting over an existing wall that has been previously painted in oil, then you must use an oil primer. You can then apply a base coat of water-based or oil-based paint. (This is the only time you can apply water-based paint over an oil-based product. The properties of oil-based primers allow latex paint to stick.)

It is more difficult to get good solid coverage with dark paint colors. If your base coat is a dark color, tint the primer with a bit of the paint. This will help get good color coverage with fewer coats of paint.

glazing liquids and colored glazes

Glazing liquid is a clear medium that is added to paint to slow down the drying time of the paint so that you can apply paint finishes to a surface. It also makes the paint translucent.

Oil-based glazing liquid is yellowish and thick, whereas water-based glazing liquid is milky and thin. Both are translucent when rubbed over a surface and when mixed with paint will not change the color of the paint.

To make a colored glaze, pour glazing liquid and paint into a container and mix well. Water-based glazing liquid is white but dries clear. It does not change the color of the paint. The more paint you add to the glazing liquid, the less translucent the colored glaze will be and the faster the drying time.

Right: Paint versus colored glaze. This board has a white base coat. The right side has 2 coats of red paint for a solid (opaque) coverage. We used red-colored glaze on the left side to create a strié effect. Its translucent quality allows the white base coat to show through.

Water-based glazing liquid must be used with latex and acrylic (water-based) paints, and oil-based glazing liquid used with oil paint. We refer to the mixture of glazing liquid and paint as a colored glaze. When a colored glaze is required in any of the projects in this book you will find a recipe that tells you the ratio of glazing liquid and paint to mix together.

varnish or top coat

note to mom or dad

Varnishes, especially the oil-based variety, are toxic. This is an adult job. Wear a mask and work in a well-ventilated area.

There are many names and products available that can be used as a protective coating for paint: urethane, polyurethane, top coat, clear coat, and varnish. For consistency I have used the term *varnish* throughout this book. Oil-based varnish has a yellow tint and will affect the final color of the surface it covers. Water-based varnish, the toughest being acrylic, dries clear. As with paint, oil varnish goes over oil- or water-based paint, but water-based varnish will not stick to oil paint.

Varnish comes in matte, semigloss, and gloss sheens. A matte sheen is the least slippery, and the water-based varieties will not alter the surface color. A high-gloss sheen will make the colors underneath appear darker, and this sheen also adds realistic depth to a paint effect such as faux marble.

A protective top coat of varnish is necessary only on surfaces that take a great deal of wear and tear, such as floors. I recommend at least 4 coats for floors. Let each coat dry before adding the next one. Sand lightly between coats, and wipe away the sanding dust with a tack cloth. Use either a varnish brush or a foam brush to eliminate brushstrokes. Let the floor cure for a week if possible before returning furniture to the room. It will feel dry to the touch almost immediately, but it takes longer for the acrylic resins to harden.

tools

I use all kinds of tools when I'm decorating. Some are specialty tools that can be expensive, but there are always cheaper alternatives that will work, and you will find them listed among the materials and tools in the project instructions.

Take proper care of your tools and they will last a long time. If you have been using an oil-based product, you will first have to remove the paint with paint thinner and then wash with soap and water. Synthetic latex brushes require only soap and water. Rinse well; then squeeze, shake, or wipe off any excess moisture. Let dry properly before you use them again. Specialty brushes, which are expensive, are traditionally made from natural hair. They need to be looked after as well as your own hair or the bristles will split. Wash them with soap and water, and occasionally use hair conditioner to keep the bristles from drying out.

note to mom or dad

Preparation for all surfaces is important. For big jobs, I suggest you do the prep work one weekend and enjoy the paint project the following weekend.

how to paint a room

Prepare * Prime * Base Coat * Painted Finish * Top Coat

When painting, always work from the top down.

1. Repair and sand all the surfaces to be painted: ceiling, walls, trim, doors, and floor.

2. Prime all areas that have been repaired and any raw surface—wood or drywall.

3. Paint and finish ceilings first.

4. Paint base coats and painted effect on walls.

5. Paint trim and doors when walls are completely dry.

6. Paint or stain the floor last.

preparing walls for paint

It's not necessary to remove all the paint, but you must smooth out any old dried drips and loose paint chips. Here we are using a sanding sponge to flatten out the paint drips on this old headboard. Then the smooth board is primed with an oil-based primer.

Any wallpaper should be removed using either wallpaper remover gels or a commercial steamer. Steamers expel very hot water; wear work gloves and use care not to burn yourself. You can also carefully gouge the surface of the paper with the edge of a spatula—you don't want to scar the wall underneath; just make random rips. Then soak the walls with a wet sponge and start scraping. A combination of these methods works best for stubborn jobs.

For all walls, wipe away any dust or cobwebs and wash the walls down with either trisodium phosphate (TSP) or vinegar and water to remove any surface grease or wallpaper residue.

To repair large cracks or holes, first brush away any loose plaster and debris and then fill in the space with a ready-mixed filler. If the hole is deep, it is better to fill in thin layers, allowing each layer to dry before adding the next until you are flush to the wall. This will make a sturdier, shrink-resistant mending job. You will need a scraper, fine-grade sandpaper, and a rag. Once all the plastered areas are dry, lightly sand over the surface to make sure the area is smooth. The plaster used for repairing cracks and holes must be primed, even if the rest of the wall surface does not require priming. Otherwise these spots will show through the fresh coat of paint.

Walls covered in wood paneling or wood veneer that is awkward to remove can be painted over to create a fresh new look. Repair any holes or cracks with wood filler, let dry, and sand smooth. The wood paneling must first be sealed with wood primer to halt any knots, stain, or old varnish from coming through the new top coat. A light sanding is required to buff up the surface and then a high-adhesion primer should be used.

note: there is no need to prime if you plan to paint a color over walls that have previously been coated in a light shade and are clean and in good condition. (If the existing paint is oil based and you want to use latex, then you must use an oil-based primer; see Primers, page 17.)

If you are changing the paint color from dark to light, a prime coat will ensure that you get good coverage without having to apply many layers of paint.

applying a base coat

When painting the ceiling, you may use ceiling paint unless you are going to apply a paint effect on the ceiling. Ceiling paint has a matte finish and is more absorbent and less durable than regular paint. Use an extension pole for your roller as it's easier to make long, even strokes.

When painting the walls, if you find it difficult to paint a clean edge, protect trim, baseboards, and ceiling with low-tack painter's tape. For an even, solid base coat and to avoid paint drips, paint buildup, and leaking under the tape, it's best to apply 2 thin coats of paint rather than 1 thick coat. Wait for the first coat to dry before adding the second coat, 2 to 4 hours depending on the heat and humidity. Begin with a brush that has a slanted tip and cut in around corners and edges. Use a roller to fill in the wall. Work in 3- or 4-foot sections starting at the top of the wall. Apply paint in parallel bands using slightly crisscrossed strokes so that roller lines are eliminated.

For clean edges:

1. Use low-tack painter's tape and press down hard along the edges with your fingers.

2. To avoid paint leaking under the tape, brush the paint from the tape out. Apply the paint in thin coats.

3. Remove the tape slowly, pulling it back on itself.

applying a paint effect (paint finish or faux finish)

The sign of a professional paint finish is that no one can tell the tools used to create the effect. This magical feat is not difficult to attain if you follow a few guidelines.

Start with colors that are similar in shade and tone for your base coat and glaze coat so that the effect will be subtle and any mistakes invisible. Go back over your work either dabbing softly with a rag or tickling the surface with a softening brush to blur or erase unwanted lines and brushstrokes. If you are simulating the look of a material such as wood planks or panels, tape off sections and work on them separately as they would appear if real. Add shadow and highlight lines to give the illusion of dimension. This simple addition is the cornerstone of trompe l'oeil, which literally means "to trick the eye" (see Sky and Skylight, page 53).

Lap lines are lines created when the colored glaze dries before you have had the chance to go back over it with a rag, brush, or other tool that is creating the paint effect. They spoil the overall look of your wall. Avoid lap lines by keeping a wet edge. Work in small sections, about 3 feet square. Start at the top of the wall, apply the glaze, work the technique, and then apply more glaze to the section directly below, overlapping the wet edge. Work the overlap first and then continue in this manner. If an edge dries before you get to it, add more glaze to open it up. It is most helpful to work with a partner, one applying the glaze and the other creating the effect.

preparing furniture for paint

Whether you have unearthed a great find at a yard sale or choose to give new life to an old piece you already have, these tips will ensure a lasting result. Note that it is not always necessary to strip all the paint or varnish from a piece of wood furniture. If it's in good repair, sand away any loose or chipped paint until you have a clean smooth surface. Apply an oil-based primer, unless you are sure the old paint is latex, and then apply your new paint finish. Drying time for oil primer is 12 hours, water-based primer 4 hours.

You can paint over laminates, but you must first sand the smooth surface to rough it up. Repair the nail holes as for wood and then apply a coat of high-adhesion primer.

Replace rusted or broken hardware. If the new hardware is a different size, fill in any noticeable depressions in the wood's surface with wood filler and sand smooth. If possible, use the same nail or screw holes.

When filling in holes or small splits in wood, use a wire brush to clear away any loose debris and dirt from the opening. Spread wood filler into the opening with a small spatula or putty knife until it is flush with the surface. Let dry. Sand lightly. If the filler shrinks, top up the opening with more filler, let dry, and sand again. Seal repair work with shellac or primer.

note to mom or dad

Stripping paint is an adult activity. The chemical fumes and sanding dust are toxic. Be sure to wear safety goggles, a proper mask, and work gloves. Work in a well-ventilated area away from children and pets.

stripping paint from furniture

If you choose to strip away all the paint or varnish from a piece of furniture, there are a few different methods to consider. They all have their place, but caution should always be used when working with harsh chemicals. Wear protective work gloves (not latex) and a mask, as the fumes are toxic.

Chemical baths or dips can be used for large projects or pieces that have intricate carving. This is done by a professional furniture stripper. But this method dries out the glues and may permanently alter the smooth workings of drawers and doors.

Wood burners can successfully remove thick layers of paint, but care must be taken not to damage the wood as the burner becomes very hot. If you want to get down to raw wood, it is much faster, and in some cases safer, to use a commercial chemical stripper. For a dresser, take drawers out and remove the hardware. Brush on chemical stripper and let it sit for 2 to 3 minutes. Remove the residue with a scraper. Use even pressure when scraping. If you press too hard you may dent the wood. Add another coat of stripper if needed. To remove hard-to-reach paint from cracks and crevices, brush on stripper, and rub with a stripping pad. Sand the surface and wipe clean. Make sure the surface is clear of any chemical residue.

sanding tips

warning: If your furniture piece is over twenty years old, and you are not sure what type of paint has been applied, it may have lead in it. It is safer and easier to chemically strip the paint away (see Stripping Paint from Furniture, page 24).

1. Sandpaper comes in different grades. Use the coarsest grade of paper to smooth down very rough or poorly finished wood pieces. Medium and fine grades are adequate for most jobs. Fine grade is used for the final touch before painting and in between coats. Sandpaper is sold in sheets. It clogs quickly, so have a good supply.

2. To make your sanding job easier, wrap a sheet of sandpaper around a block of wood. This gives you something to grip, and the pressure on each sanding stroke will be even.

3. There are spongy sanding blocks available that are easy to use and can be rinsed clean of dust. They have a sharp edge for reaching into corners and cracks.

4. When sanding wood, always move with the grain as much as possible to avoid scratching and blurring the surface.

5. Wipe away the sanding dust with a soft, clean, lint-free rag or tack cloth. A tack cloth is permeated with a sticky substance that dust adheres to, making cleanup a breeze. Don't press down too hard when you wipe up the sanding dust or the stickiness will stay behind on your surface.

painting tips for furniture

dressers

1. Remove the drawers. Remove hardware.

2. Use a bristle or sponge brush to apply the paint.

3. Apply paint in the direction of the wood grain. If there is no grain, work as if there were, running the length of the boards. To avoid drips, apply 2 thin coats. Let the first coat dry before adding the second.

4. Replace either new or renewed hardware.

chairs

1. Use a bristle or sponge brush (a bristle brush will get into the crevices and around spindles better).

2. Turn the chair upside down and paint the legs first, moving toward the seat. Then paint the bottom of the seat. To avoid drips, apply the paint in thin coats.

3. When the legs are dry, turn the chair right side up and finish painting from the top down to the seat. Paint the seat last.

tables

1. Use a bristle or sponge brush.

2. Turn the table upside down. Paint the legs first, then the undersurface of the tabletop, applying the paint in thin coats.

3. When dry, flip over and paint the tabletop and edges.

children's bedrooms

A child's bedroom is the place where he or she will spend an enormous amount of time. And the process of helping your children design and decorate their rooms is as important as the results, even if the results reflect more their taste than yours.

Paint is the most practical and inexpensive way to add character and fun to your children's rooms. Color can be soothing or stimulating, and the effect is instant. Even if you do not change the furnishings or fabrics, just a fresh new color on the walls will bring about a huge change. The great thing about paint is that it can be covered over easily with a coat of primer and the room reinvented with a fresh color. If you are a child reading this, then this is the best argument to give your parents when persuading them to go along with your color scheme.

Children's bedrooms evolve from the nursery to the "hangout." You will be amazed at how quickly these years fly by, but even so, each stage of a child's growth will entail different requirements for their rooms. A baby's room is solely your responsibility, inspired by your own ideas for a nurturing environment. Once your little one has climbed out of the crib a dozen times, then it is time for a bed, and toy storage becomes one of your biggest dilemmas. That handful of cuddly toys has now grown into boxes of building blocks, movable toys, crayons, and puzzle pieces. Your child's room now needs to be both stimulating for play as well as comforting for naps and bedtime.

As soon as children are off to school, their parents' influence begins to decline. Children will now have best friends whose opinions carry more weight than yours, and their blossoming independence means more input into their own color schemes, display areas, and storage. By the time they are teenagers, their bedroom doors are usually shut tight. This will be the last time that you will decorate your child's room. I recommend going with the flow and helping teens visualize their own personal style—even if you are rarely invited in to enjoy the results.

o v e r
the rainbow

Even an adult is filled with wonder at the sight of a rainbow.
It is a visible manifestation of the color spectrum starting with red, then moving through orange, yellow, green, blue, and violet at the opposite end. What could be more magical for a new baby than rainbow walls? Thinned-down yellow, blue, and red bands of paint were blended together as a backdrop for a pattern of stenciled angels. Every mother believes that her new baby is an angel, and it's an easy theme to build upon. Here we fashioned child-sized hangers using fiberboard and a cherub stencil. Rather than tucked away in a cupboard, these decorate the walls hung along a row of wooden pegs.

rainbow walls

MATERIALS AND TOOLS

*white, yellow, pale blue, and pink latex
paint, satin*

roller and paint tray

low-tack painter's tape

water-based glazing liquid

3 mixing containers

three 4" paintbrushes

RECIPE

1 part latex paint

2 parts water-based glazing liquid

This beautiful rainbow effect is produced by color-washing the walls with only three colors. By overlapping the colors I ended up with five shades, making a realistic spectrum. The paint was mixed with glaze to slow down the drying time so that I could blend the edges, and the glaze also makes the colors more translucent and ethereal. A brother or sister can help with the stenciling and will feel he or she is taking an important part in the preparations for the new arrival.

For best results, prepare your surface following the instructions in the Start Right chapter, pages 14–27.

step 1 Apply 2 coats of white base coat and let dry for 4 hours. Apply low-tack tape to protect adjacent walls and the ceiling.

step 2 Mix your colored glazes.

step 3 (Shot 1) Starting at the bottom of the wall, apply your yellow glaze first with a wide paintbrush. Put very little on, crisscrossing, and blend together lightly to get rid of brushstrokes. Some areas should be a little stronger than others. Cover approximately one-third of the height of the wall.

step 4 (Shot 2) Apply the blue glaze in the same manner, starting at the ceiling and working down one-third of the wall, leaving 2–3 feet in the middle. The bands of color shouldn't be even.

step 5 (Shot 3) For the middle strip, apply the pink glaze following the same instructions, and as you move up and down the wall, overlap the blue and the yellow. The overlapped bits will change color slightly (for example, blue and pink will turn to lilac, and pink and yellow will make a soft orange), creating the rainbow effect. Let dry.

alternate method

You may apply the colored glazes from the top of the wall down if you want to maintain a wet edge. The colors will blend together rather than overlap each other.

cherub stencil

MATERIALS AND TOOLS

low-tack painter's tape

periwinkle blue artist's acrylic paint

pearlescent paint

paper plate

cherub stencil (see Resources)

nonpermanent spray adhesive

medium stencil brush

paper towel

note to mom or dad
Kids love to stencil, but make sure the brush is "dry."
Also, spray and position the stencil for your child.

step 1   Decide where on the walls you want to place the stenciled angels and mark the positions with pieces of low-tack tape.

step 2   Put an equal dab of each paint onto the plate and mix them together. Spray the back of the stencil with adhesive and stick into position on the wall, removing the tape as you do.

step 3   Dip the stencil brush into the paint and remove the excess paint onto a paper towel. The brush should be almost dry.

step 4   (*Shot 1*) Fill in the stencil using a pouncing and a swirling motion with the brush.

step 5   Remove the stencil and wipe off any paint that may have seeped through onto the back. Reposition and continue stenciling.

1

angel coat hangers

These angelic hangers are meant to be seen, so attach a row of hooks or pegs to the wall. Make three or four hangers and paint them different colors that will complement your nursery. They also make a thoughtful and unique gift for a new mom.

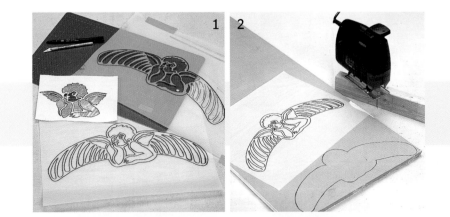

MATERIALS AND TOOLS

cherub stencil (see Resources)

photocopier

pencil

scissors

medium-density fiberboard (MDF) or
    plywood

jigsaw

primer

blue and white latex paint, satin

2″ paintbrush

cutting mat

Mylar

marker

X-acto knife

nonpermanent spray adhesive

small stencil brush

wooden hanger

hammer

nails, optional

contact cement

step 1   (Shot 1) Enlarge the cherub on a photocopier so that it is approximately 6″ high. Here the wings are not big enough, so I extended them freehand so that the length from tip to tip is 16″. Draw in feather lines.

step 2   (Shot 2) Cut out your cherub form, leaving ½″ border all around. Use this as a template to trace onto the MDF. Cut out the shape with a jigsaw.

step 3   (Shot 3) Apply primer and 2 coats of blue base coat to the cutout MDF form and let dry.

step 4   Make the cherub stencil as follows: Place the photocopy on the cutting board under a sheet of Mylar. Trace the image using a fine marker. Remove the photocopy and cut out the stencil with a sharp knife.

step 5   (Shot 4) Spray adhesive onto the back of the stencil and position it onto the painted cherub form. Using the stencil brush and white paint, fill in the stencil.

step 6   (Shot 5) Cut down a wooden hanger so that there is 1½″ of wood left attached to the wire. Paint the same blue as the MDF cherub. Let dry. Attach the wire hanger to the back of the cherub using finishing nails and contact cement.

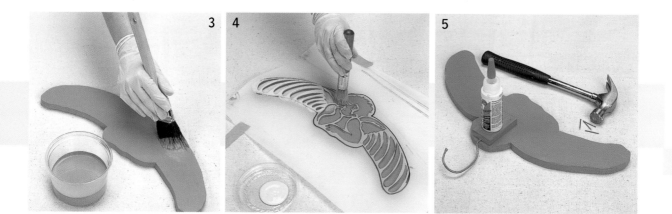

3   4   5

baby boy

A nursery's decor is as much about your state of mind as it is about the baby's. You will be spending many hours here feeding and changing your baby, so use a palette of soothing tones that will keep you as relaxed as your little one. The walls for this baby boy were painted in a soft beige, accented in navy blue. Jake's mom already had a collection of teddy bears, so we carried on the theme by painting paw prints over the wall. This neutral decor can be adapted easily with more stimulating accessories as the baby grows.

teddy paw prints

Painting paw prints can be done in many ways: Stamping, stenciling, or freehand painting are all possibilities. The idea is to keep all the paw prints similar and make sure they are angled in a realistic walking pattern. Here I first stenciled in a very light outline and removed the stencil. Then, with a stencil brush, I pounced each pad so that the bristles left behind a furry border. To make it look more authentic, add a little white and brown as a highlight on one side of each pad, which will make the paw look rounded.

MATERIALS AND TOOLS

Mylar

marker

X-acto knife

low-tack painter's tape

spray adhesive

dark brown, rusty brown, and white acrylic paint

plastic plate

3 medium stencil brushes

paper towel

step 1   Make a paw print stencil by drawing a simple design onto the Mylar with the marker. Use the X-acto knife to cut out the shape.

step 2   Decide on the pattern the paw prints are going to take along the wall and mark it off with low-tack tape.

step 3   (*Shot 1*) Use spray adhesive or tape to stick the stencil into position on the wall. Put blobs of dark and rusty brown paint on the plate. Dip a stencil brush into the dark brown, then remove the excess paint with a paper towel. Fill in the stencil with a very light layer of paint by pouncing the flat tip of the stencil brush lightly against the surface. Move the stencil to the next position and fill in a light impression. Complete the remainder of the paw pattern in this manner.

step 4   (*Shot 2*) Mix the two brown paints together on the plate. To make the paw prints look furry, remove the stencil and pounce over the prints to blur the edges. Let dry.

step 5   (*Shot 3*) Finish off by mixing a little white paint with the brown and pounce lightly onto one side of each pad. This will add realistic definition to the paw prints.

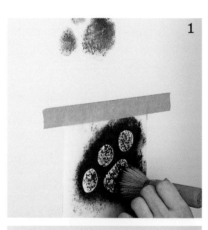

primary colors

The inspiration for this happy nursery came from fabric designed by one of my favorite style mavens, Tricia Guild. It is aptly named "Mad Hatter" (see Resources, page 174, for Designer's Guild fabric). To build on the theme a window valance was fashioned to represent a jester's collar or a row of pointed flags. The walls were glazed in tones of red, orange, and yellow, blended with a rag to soften the look. Old kitchen cabinets are the perfect storage solution for this tiny room and were painted to complement the circus theme. The owner, a clever designer in her own right, transformed a carpenter's workbench into a changing table just the right height for two tall parents to care for their new baby.

jester valance

Designer fabrics can be costly, but you only need a little to make a big impact. This Designer's Guild pattern was cut into two rows of triangles and backed with a less-expensive matching solid green cotton. A rod pocket was sewn down the middle, the valance slipped over a wooden rod, and the upper triangles flipped forward to create an amusing casual window topper.

colorwashed walls

The nursery walls were colorwashed with orange and yellow glaze over a cream base coat. The two colors were applied at the same time with a 4″ brush and the brush strokes were blended out with a folded rag. This is great for a child's room, as it is durable and long-lasting.

custom wood changing table

Before assembling the workbench, measure the height and length and cut the wood to fit your space. If you want more height, add "feet" to the uprights as we did here with fence-post finials. Sand the wood smooth, making sure to round off the edges and corners. When assembling the table, glue plugs or mushroom caps over the screws to protect the baby from scratches. Choose a changing pad with raised sides and adhere the pad to the tabletop with Velcro strips nailed down for added holding strength and maximum safety.

A color wash of 1 part latex paint and 1 part water was used to stain the wood in colors that match the cabinets.

good. knight

Nine-year-old Evan's fascination for medieval knights was the inspiration behind the decoration of his bedroom. He had just inherited the family guest room as his own room, and the first task was to remove the floral wallpaper. I did not want to make the medieval theme too childish, so we searched through books on English history for a series of ancestral shields. These were simplified and cut into stencils. Using metallic paints, we stenciled them over wide, color-washed stripes. Evan suffers from asthma and has mild allergies. To help eliminate dust and mold, we removed his wall-to-wall carpet and replaced it with a "floating" cork floor. The wooden blinds are an ideal alternative to curtains.

cork floor

I am a huge fan of cork flooring because it is durable, warm underfoot, and easy to keep clean. It's also a fabulous alternative to carpeting for children with allergies. Cork flooring is available in tiles or panels and can be installed prestained and presealed. The wide variety of patterns offers you great design flexibility. It's also an environmentally friendly product as it is produced from the bark of the cork oak tree grown across Portugal. The bark is stripped but the tree left standing, and the bark grows back within nine years.

striped walls with shield stenciling

With paint and a stencil you can make a one-of-a-kind wall finish to build on any theme. These stripes were easily fashioned using a kitchen sponge and colored glaze. If you can't find a stencil you like, make your own by copying an image onto Mylar. Use a cutting board and a sharp X-acto knife to make clean cutting lines. When cutting around curves, turn the Mylar and hold the knife steady, instead of moving the X-acto knife.

MATERIALS AND TOOLS

yellow and medium green latex paint,
    satin

roller and paint tray

3" paintbrush

ruler and pencil

chalk line

low-tack painter's tape

water-based glazing liquid

mixing container

kitchen sponge

stencil

or

Mylar, marker, X-acto knife, cutting
    pad (if making your own stencil)

adhesive

light and dark gray stencil paint

small foam roller and paint tray

note to mom or dad

To avoid paint leaking under the tape, press the tape down firmly and apply a thin coat of paint over and away from the tape line (see Applying a Base Coat, page 22).

For best results, prepare your surface following the instructions in the Start Right chapter, page 14–27.

step 1   Apply 2 coats of yellow base coat to the walls and let dry for 4 hours.

step 2   (Shot 1) Use the ruler, pencil, and chalk line to divide the wall into 12" vertical stripes. Using the low-tack tape, tape off alternate stripes, running the tape along the outside of the lines of the stripes to be painted. It's normal for these stripes to now look fatter than the other stripes. Mark an X with tape on the stripes not to be painted.

1 part latex paint

2 parts water-based glazing liquid

step 3   (*Shot 2*) Mix the green glaze. Dampen a kitchen
        sponge with water and wring it out thoroughly. Dip
        the sponge into the glaze and wash the color onto
        the stripes, creating a cloudy effect. Let dry and
        remove the tape.

step 4   (*Shot 3*) Decide where you want the stencil images to
        go. We alternated first three, then two shields on
        the green stripes all around the room. Spray the
        back of the stencil and stick it into position. Fill in
        with light and dark gray stencil paint at the same
        time with a roller. For a more realistic effect try
        using metallic paint.

step 5   Remove stencil and repeat the pattern around the
        room.

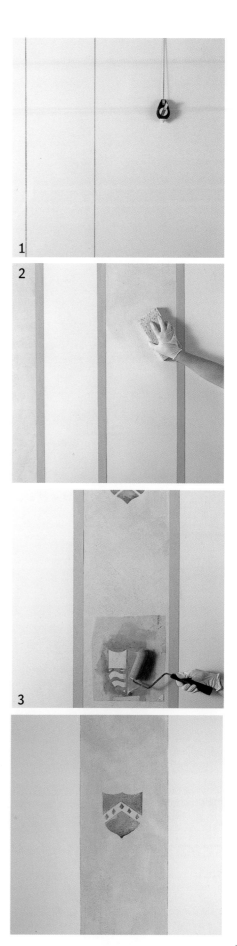

purple haze

Teens have strong color preferences, one of the most popular
being purple, a color that horrifies many parents. I compromised in Haley's bedroom by rolling shades of pearlized lilac and mauve glaze over a pale blue base coat. Most fifteen-year-olds do little alone, so with a team of her friends we painted a stunning trompe l'oeil skylight. The choice of window treatment was influenced by the hippies of the 1960s—unheard of by Haley! Purple sheers were first hung onto metal curtain rods and then silk flowers and straws were threaded together with transparent thread. I also created an elaborate ceiling that was not only a painted sky but a skylight as well. It took a weekend to accomplish, but the effect is fabulous. Decorating Haley's room was a wonderful experience as I was allowed a glimpse into the giggling, joyous world of these young ladies.

flowers and sheers

This window treatment is for the kids to make and adds to the "flower power" feeling of the room. Lengths of silk string were threaded through drinking straws, separated by inexpensive silk flowers and leaves that are wired into place. The straws keep the thread hanging straight. Cup hooks were screwed 8 inches apart into a white dowel the width of the window. The decorated strings are tied to the hooks. For privacy and color, purple sheers were first hung at the window, and the white dowel with the flowers and straws was secured in front of the sheers from wall hooks. Very cool!

color blending

There are many methods of blending colors. This technique uses a specially designed roller and tray so that you can apply two colors at the same time. It's great fun and moves along quickly. Choose two colors that have a similar tone. Here I used two new pearlescent shades that create a delicate shimmer on the surface.

MATERIALS AND TOOLS

pale pink latex paint, satin

roller and paint tray

low-tack painter's tape

lavender and lilac pearlescent latex paint

double roller and split paint tray (see Resources)

For best results, prepare your surface following the instructions in the Start Right chapter, pages 14–27.

step 1   Apply 2 coats of pale pink base coat and let dry for 4 hours.

step 2   Work on one wall at a time. Tape off the edges of the adjacent walls. When the wall is complete and dry, remove the tape and reposition for the next wall. This will ensure clean corners.

step 3   (Shot 1) In the split tray, pour lavender pearlescent paint in one side and lilac in the other. Load the divided roller with the 2 paints.

step 4   (Shots 2 and 3) Roll the paint onto the wall in wide arcs moving back and forth without removing the roller from the wall. Go over the surface in different directions, removing roller marks and blending the colors together until the whole surface is covered. Be careful

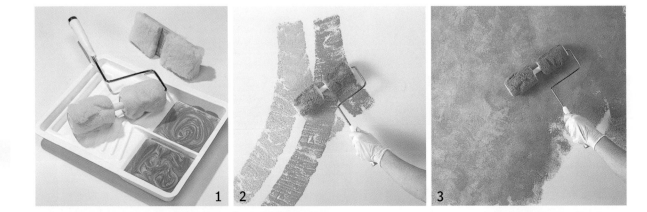

1   2   3

not to overblend, because the colors will become muddy. Most of these kits come with a special edging tool so that you can get into the corners neatly. Let dry.

step 5   Remove the tape and reposition to do the next wall.

sky and skylight

note to mom or dad
This is a great project to do along with teens. You can all take turns climbing the ladder and taking much needed neck breaks.

This realistic-looking sky is painted in the same speedy manner as the effect on the walls. Here the colors are applied in solid paint, and the paint is applied in an uneven texture. Over the white base coat of the ceiling, I masked off the skylight frames (follow the pattern in the picture). Light blue and white paint was rolled onto the ceiling using a split tray and double roller. The colors blend together, creating a blue and white mottled background for the sky. Next the clouds are added using the roller in thicker patches of white, and the edges can be softened with a sea sponge. Make sure they are all moving in the same direction as if being blown by the wind.

For the skylight I removed the tape, retaped half the width of each frame, and painted in the gray shadow lines. Be careful not to make the bands too thin. I finished off the ceiling with a deep aqua-colored border, which separates the ceiling from the walls.

cute to cool

There comes a time in every young girl's life when the cute, pretty decor of her bedroom needs to be replaced with a cool space. It seems to happen overnight at the same time your daughter's dolls are replaced with nail varnish, hair accessories, clothing, and, of course, gossip and giggles about the latest pop star and that handsome eleven-year-old boy in her class. In this room, I helped Linnet remove her floral wallpaper, fluffy curtains, and wall-to-wall carpet. She told me that blue was the coolest color, so we used tones from dark to light in an ombré effect down the walls. The hardwood floor was stripped, cleaned, and painted a vibrant blue and was finished with huge daisies stenciled over the surface. Linnet and I found an old hospital table in her attic, and after receiving permission from her mom, we turned it into a bedside table decorated in floating memorabilia.

before

Flowery wallpaper and frilly curtains were the favorite decor when Linnet was young, but as she grew up, the look had to change.

ombré walls

Ombré is the effect created when one color moves seamlessly into another, often seen in a rainbow. Here we used the sea as an example, where the dark blue grows lighter and blends into different tones of blue. To achieve this look the walls are first coated in a layer of wet glaze, then colors are blended over the surface with kitchen sponges.

MATERIALS AND TOOLS

white latex paint, satin

roller and paint tray

low-tack painter's tape

water-based glazing liquid

roller and paint tray

pale turquoise blue, medium blue, and deep blue latex paint, satin

3 mixing containers

3 foam rollers and paint trays

3 kitchen sponges

RECIPE

1 part latex paint

1 part water-based glazing liquid

For best results, prepare your surface following the instructions in the Start Right chapter, pages 14–27.

step 1 Apply 2 coats of white base coat and let dry for 4 hours.

step 2 Work on one wall at a time. Tape off each wall as you do it to ensure neat edges.

step 3 Mix the 3 blue glazes.

step 4 (Shot 1) Apply a layer of clear latex glaze to the wall with a roller.

step 5 (Shot 2) While the glaze is still wet, start from the top of the wall and apply the palest blue glaze with a foam roller to about one-third of the way down the wall. Your stop line doesn't have to be perfectly straight, because the next color is going to blend into it.

step 6 (Shot 3) Dab the color with the sponge to blur any roller marks. Don't overdo it as you don't want too much paint to come off. Seeing some of the white wall, though, will give the finish a light airy feeling.

1 2 3 4

step 7 *(Shot 4)* Keep the bottom edge of the applied pale blue glaze quite thick (a wet edge). Apply the medium blue with a clean foam roller to the middle third of the wall. Don't touch the upper part until you have the rest applied, and then just overlap by about 4″. With a clean sponge, first blend the lap line to get rid of any seam marks and then blend the rest to blur any roller marks.

step 8 If the glaze is drying out on the lower third of the wall, apply more clear glaze. Roll and sponge the darkest blue glaze to the lower third as in step 5. Let dry.

bed table

While rooting around in Linnet's attic, we found an old hospital table the perfect shape and size for a bedside table. We turned the top into a "floating" collage of her favorite memories. We collected old concert tickets, photos, and jewelry and glued them in a random pattern over a freshly painted surface. Instead of just varnishing over the top— the traditional decoupage method, I used epoxy varnish, which is equivalent to about 50 coats of standard varnish. This gives the illusion that the collection is suspended in the clear medium. The epoxy varnish is toxic, so send the children out of the room, wear a mask, and make sure the area is well ventilated. (It's best to apply epoxy varnish outdoors if possible.)

daisy floor

MATERIALS AND TOOLS

- white poster board
- marker
- X-acto knife
- stencil adhesive
- low-tack painter's tape
- white latex paint, satin
- 2 small foam rollers and paint trays
- pearlescent pink latex paint
- satin acrylic varnish
- large foam roller

note to mom or dad:
X-acto knives are very sharp, but children can help with the rest of the floor.

The old carpet in Linnet's room was removed to reveal a hardwood floor. Once sanded, washed, and primed, it was painted a cheerful blue. There is something about the simplicity of the daisy that makes this flower a constant inspiration to designers. Popular in the 1960s on clothing, the daisy pattern is now depicted everywhere from fashion items to home furnishings. I cut large daisy stencils from sheets of poster board, and by rolling white paint over the cutouts, a garden of scattered daisies created a groovy floor.

step 1   *(Shot 1)* Draw 2 or 3 simple daisy shapes of varying sizes onto pieces of poster board. Include a circle in the middle of each daisy. Cut out each daisy and the center circle with a sharp knife. Using the circle as a template, cut another circle approximately ½" larger.

step 2   *(Shot 2)* Use the adhesive or low-tack tape to secure the outside of the daisy stencil in position on the floor. Spray the back of the *larger* circle with adhesive and place it in the center of the daisy. Fill in the daisy with the white paint. Remove the stencil and circle and let dry.

step 3   *(Shot 3)* Using the inside of the stencil cutout, position it over the white painted daisy. Fill in the small center hole with the pearlescent paint.

step 4   Once all the daisies are dry, apply 3 coats of varnish for sheen and protection.

honky-tonk

Fuchsia and chartreuse may not be your chosen color palette
for a formal living room, but for a funky young girl's bedroom it was an instant hit. She wanted a room that was bright and colorful, a space where she could impress her friends, listen to music, and just "hang." The color palette and patterns I chose were inspired by a "rock and roll" hotel in London. The designer of the hotel had used expensive fur trim on the walls, highlighted with fuchsia feather boas. This was beyond our budget, so I re-created the London style with paint and texture. The walls were painted in chartreuse green with a leopard-print border trimmed with fuchsia. Using mirrored Con-Tact paper, we made a heart-shaped headboard reminiscent of a disco ball and dressed the room with bright colors and animal prints.

glittery curtains

Today ready-made sheers are easily available and inexpensive. They are usually plain fabric, but you can personalize them by adding your own pattern and texture. This can be achieved with paint, other fabrics, borders and trims, or, in this case, paper. Here two different sheers with tab tops were hung from the same rod. Squares of mirrored Con-Tact paper were stuck randomly over the white sheers and the silver sheers hang in the back. The paper must be removed before washing.

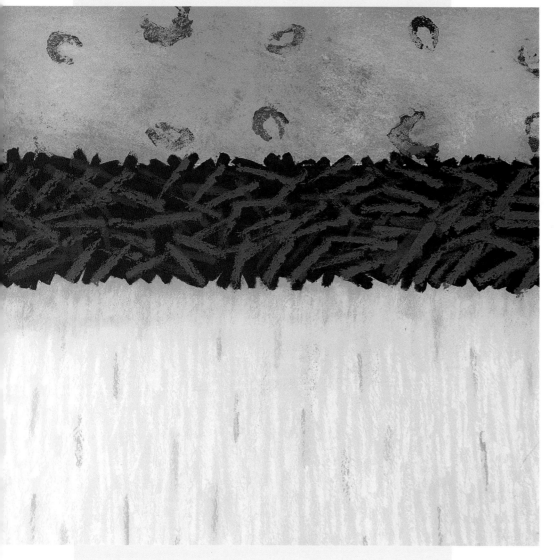

A wonderful and imaginative mix of colors and textures was applied to Sophy's bedroom walls, but it was all done with paint, so it will be easy to change when she grows tired of it. This exotic look is not for the faint of heart—be sure to get Mom's permission first. Use a level and chalk line to divide the wall into three sections: the upper leopard border, the faux feather band, and the grassy main wall.

grass walls

MATERIALS AND TOOLS

ruler

chalk line and level

low-tack painter's tape

grass green latex paint, satin

roller and paint tray

white and 2 other shades of grass green latex paint, satin

3 or 4 mixing containers

3 or 4 small nap rollers and paint trays

For best results, prepare your surface following the instructions in the Start Right chapter, pages 14–27.

step 1 Divide the wall using a ruler, chalk line, and level. The top border is 18″ deep and the fur rail is 6″ deep. Tape off below the top line and above the bottom line.

step 2 Apply 2 coats of medium green base coat to the area below the lower chalk line. (The brown base for the leopard print border is painted at the same time. See page 64.)

step 3 (*Shot 1*) To make the grass effect, add small amounts of white paint to the various shades of green in different containers to make 3 or 4 different greens in all. Apply the first color to a small roller. Holding the roller with the sleeve parallel to the wall, dab the length of the sleeve against the wall and repeat all over, creating vertical rectangular marks.

step 4 (*Shot 2*) Repeat step 3 with a clean roller and all the different shades of green until the wall is liberally covered with multicolored blades of grass.

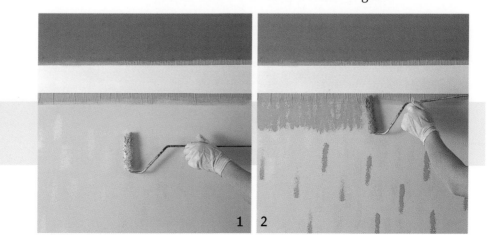

1   2

leopard-print border

MATERIALS AND TOOLS

3 shades of caramel brown latex paint,
   satin

3 small rollers and paint trays

paper towel or craft paper

marker

2″ thick upholstery foam

X-acto knife

chocolate brown latex paint, satin

note to mom or dad

Sponge stamping is easy, but take care when cutting the foam with the sharp X-acto knife.

step 1   To create the shading found in real fur, first apply 2 coats of dark caramel base coat to the upper wall border and let dry for 4 hours.

step 2   (Shot 1) Then apply the lighter color first with a fairly dry roller. Roll on in random patches along the border.

step 3   (Shot 2) Using the medium color now, roll it on again in patches, blending with the other tones of caramel.

step 4   (Shot 3) Using the marker, draw 2 or 3 irregular, elongated C shapes on the foam and cut out using the X-acto knife. Dip the foam stamp into chocolate brown paint, remove the excess onto paper towel, and apply the stamp randomly over the surface of the border. Repeat with the other sized stamps.

step 5   Make circular stamps from the foam that will fit inside the C shapes. Dip them into both light and dark caramel shades and stamp inside the chocolate C's to represent a leopard's spots. Let dry and remove all the tape.

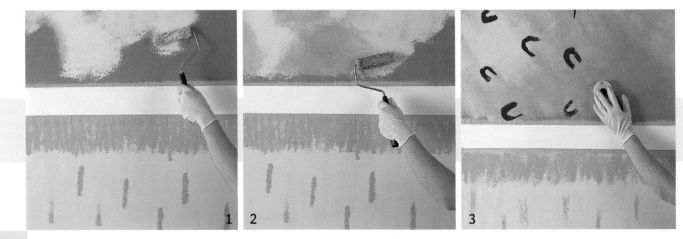

feather border

MATERIALS AND TOOLS

purply black, red, and fuchsia latex paint, satin

3 small rollers and paint trays

step 1   *(Shot 1)* Using a roller, fill in the border between the leopard print and grass walls with the deep purple paint. Create jagged edges on the border by holding the roller sleeve parallel to the wall and dabbing the paint at all angles over the top and bottom of the band of paint.

step 2   *(Shot 2)* Apply red paint to a second small roller and dab it in the same manner, randomly over the border.

step 3   *(Shot 3)* Repeat step 2 with the fuchsia paint.

heart mosaic headboard

MATERIALS AND TOOLS

³/₄″ plywood or MDF

pencil

jigsaw

fine- and medium-grade sandpaper

wood primer

black latex paint, matte

roller and paint tray

ruler and chalk line

silver reflective Con-Tact paper

scissors or a sharp knife

Inspired by a disco ball, this dazzling head-board was made using mirrored Con-Tact paper. It is important to use either smooth plywood or MDF, or the Con-Tact paper won't adhere.

step 1   (Shot 1) Draw out a heart shape on a piece of ply-wood or MDF to fit behind a bed. Here it was a twin bed, so our measurements were 47″ wide and 42″ from the bottom point to the cleavage of the heart. Cut it out with a jigsaw and sand the edges smooth. Apply 1 coat of wood primer to the front and edges.

step 2   Apply 2 coats of the matte black paint to the head-board and let dry for 4 hours or overnight.

step 3   Using the ruler and chalk line, separate the heart shape into four equal quadrants.

step 4   (Shot 2) Cut the reflective Con-Tact paper into 1″ × 2″ rectangles. Work on one quadrant at a time. Starting from the center of the heart, remove the backing and apply the rectangles as if you were laying out tiles. Leave ¹/₁₆″ space between the pieces; the black base coat will appear as a grout line.

step 5   Attach the headboard to the wall with heavy-duty wall clips and plugs, hanging it behind the bed like a large picture.

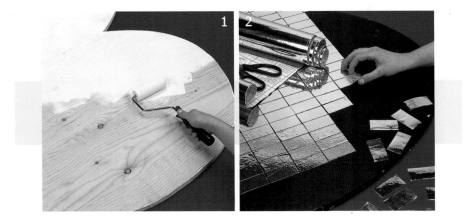

enter the dragon

Orville has a passion for karate and wanted a room that had an Eastern flavor to complement his interest. The walls were painted in a deep turquoise and then decorated with images of an oriental dragon stamped over the surface. For the ceiling I painted a bamboo design, not by hand but by using a "pattern" roller. This is a little tricky at first because of the height of a ceiling, but once you get the hang of it, it's fast and the results are fun. Because Orville was short on space, I took an old chest of drawers and cut it down to table height by removing the bottom drawer and then added wheels. We then painted the chest of drawers with a Japanese red lacquer effect. The final touch was Chinese coins called "cash" that can be found in Chinese shops, which we added around the drawer pulls. He now has a table that he can sit around with his friends, and it doubles as storage for his clothing.

patterned ceiling

MATERIALS AND TOOLS

ocher latex paint, matte
mustard latex paint, satin
patterned roller (see Resources)
extension pole
large paint tray

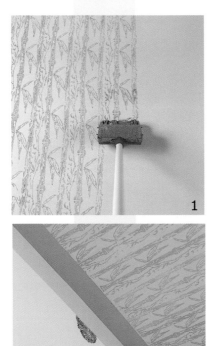

Working on a ceiling is not the easiest job, but the results can be amazing, and well worth the effort. For this effect, the patterned roller makes the design, but you need a steady stroke for it to look good. The trick is to move from one end of the ceiling to the other in a straight line—without lifting the roller! To separate the patterned ceiling from the turquoise walls, we painted a tan-colored band around the room. It looks like two shades, but this is a trick of light.

For best results, prepare your surface following the instructions in the Start Right chapter, pages 14–27.

step 1 Apply 2 coats of ocher base coat and let dry for 4 hours. You must use paint with a matte finish, as the patterned roller will slip and slide over anything glossier.

step 2 Attach the patterned roller to a long, strong, and straight extension pole.

step 3 *(Shot 1)* Load the roller with mustard paint and apply in one long continuous stroke without stopping or lifting the roller. Reload and continue to work from one end of the room to the other.

chinese chest

When you work on old furniture it is important to wash down the whole piece well to remove any dirt or grease. If the original paint is peeling, then it must be sanded down (see Preparing Furniture for Paint, page 24). Apply a coat of good primer designed to adhere to shiny surfaces. Here I applied 2 coats of Chinese red paint and then rubbed a brown glaze over the dry surface. To make the brown glaze, mix equal parts brown paint and glazing liquid. Rub it over the surface in swirls with a kitchen sponge to produce an antique effect. Let dry and apply 2 coats of high-gloss varnish for sheen and protection. For the finishing touch I added Chinese cash coins around the handle; these are available at Chinese souvenir shops.

dragon stamp

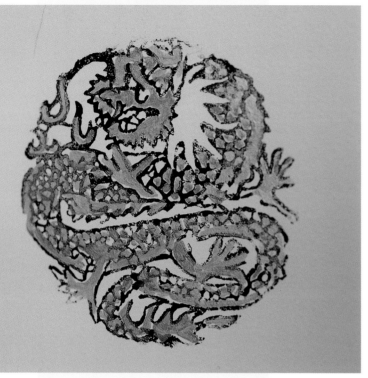

MATERIALS AND TOOLS

blank printing block for making ink stamps

pencil

tracing paper

tiny hooked chisel for gouging out designs in rubber, available at art or craft stores

block of wood or MDF

carpenter's wood glue

black latex paint, satin

ink roller

gold paint and artist's brush (optional)

Stamps are usually made of rubber and come in an enormous variety of designs. You can also buy the rubber, stick it to a block of wood, and cut out your own images. There are special tools designed to do this fine cutting, available at art suppliers.

When stamping, mark out where you want each stamp to go with masking tape. Apply very little paint to the stamp using an ink roller or a brush. Make sure the paint doesn't get into the grooves or your design will be blurry. Reapply the paint after each impression to make sure the color is uniform. We filled in the dragon design with gold paint and an artist's brush.

step 1   (*Shot 1*) Either use a ready-made stamp or make your own design. We chose an intricate dragon design. Draw or photocopy it to your desired size. Copy it onto a piece of tracing paper with a pencil.

step 2   (*Shot 2*) Place the tracing paper, pencil side down, onto the printing block. Retrace the image to transfer the pencil marks to the rubber.

step 3   (*Shot 3*) Use the tiny chisel to dig out the areas between the pencil marks, to about half the depth of the block.

step 4   Glue the carved block to a piece of wood or MDF to give it stability and to make stamping easier. Mark the center points on the 4 sides of the back of the block. These registration lines will help you to line up the stamp on the wall so that it is always straight.

step 5   (*Shot 4*) Apply the black paint evenly over the surface of the stamp with an ink roller.

step 6   Press the stamp with an even pressure onto the surface you are decorating. Pull it away cleanly to ensure a clear image.

step 7   If desired, use an artist's brush to fill in the spaces with gold paint.

caribbean
style

I love the colors and textures used on both the inside and outside of the houses in the Caribbean. When Kelly, a vivacious teenager, asked me to help her "go wild" in her bedroom, we both agreed on island style. Her walls already had a heavy coating of uneven stucco, so instead of trying to camouflage the texture, we highlighted it by rubbing a vibrant color on each wall. The choice of furnishings is extremely limited on many of the islands, so the local people use their imaginations to decorate their homes with whatever recycled products they can find. Kelly and I collected colored bottles, beads, and shells to create an eclectic rhythm in her room.

bed canopy

In the Caribbean, bed canopies are a necessity to protect sleepers from bugs, but they are also romantic. We took some inexpensive gauze and draped it over a bamboo rod suspended from the ceiling on two hooks. The fabric was cut in large zigzags and finished off with threaded shells tied onto the edges. (Beads are available from bead shops with the holes already in place.)

bottle frame

Here's a novel approach to hanging a collection of necklaces, belts, or ties. It takes a bit of carpentry skill to cut the circles for the bottles, but the decorating is fun. Tinted plaster adds its own texture, and to reinforce the Caribbean theme we embedded colored glass beads into the plaster for more panache. Whether you use wood or MDF, the board must be an inch thick to give the bottles a proper gripping surface.

MATERIALS AND TOOLS

*1" thick MDF for frame (ours is 24½"
     × 36", the width of the top and
     bottom are 6" and the sides 3")*

*glass bottles (ours have a 3" diameter
     at the bottom)*

pencil

drill

jigsaw

wood glue

2 picture hanging hooks

water-based primer

paintbrush

dark pink and ocher latex paint, matte

plaster

2 mixing containers

metal spatula

universal adhesive

caulking adhesive and caulking gun

clean, damp cloth

step 1 Using the bottom of a bottle as a template, draw 4 circles, 1" from the side edges and 3½" apart centered along the top of the frame. Drill a hole inside the circle so that you can fit in the jigsaw and then use the jigsaw to cut out the circles. Attach the hanging hooks to the back of the frame now, one on each side, as it is difficult to do once the bottles are in place.

step 2 Prime the frame, let dry 4 hours.

step 3 (Shot 1) Divide the plaster into 2 containers and tint 1 with the pink and 1 with the ocher paint. Mix well. Apply the pink plaster over the primed wood with a spatula, covering most of the white. Make it as smooth or textured as you like.

step 4 (Shot 2) While the pink plaster is still wet, spread on the ocher plaster, pulling the spatula through to mix and blend the colors. Let dry.

step 5 (Shot 3) Apply a little more pink plaster and blend with spatula. Don't overblend or you'll muddy the ocher.

step 6 (*Shot 4*) Apply glue to the bottom rim of the bottles and insert them into the holes only as far as the back of the frame.

step 7 Use the caulking gun to secure the bottles. Squeeze the caulking around the edges and in between the bottles and the board. Wipe away any excess with a damp cloth. Once the caulking is dry, paint it to match your frame.

dressed-up wire lampshade

A painted wire wastepaper basket was given a new life as a funky lampshade by adding strings of beads.

77

playful
plaid

Plaid has always been a popular choice for the soft furnish- ings in a boy's room, but why limit these Highland patterns to just fabrics? My assistant Dana helped her next-door neighbor Adam paint his bedroom walls in the bright colors of a Scottish tartan. Instead of solid color, she used a mix of paint and glaze so that the effect would be soft and translucent.

painted plaid walls

The best way to go about this project is to work out your plaid pattern on a large piece of bristol board. Draw out and color in the plaid to the size you'll want on the walls. Then use this as a template for your walls. Use a plumb line and level to ensure the lines are straight. Link up horizontal stripes with a window frame or doorway.

MATERIALS AND TOOLS

white, blue, yellow, and red latex paint, satin

2 large and 3 small rollers and paint trays

bristol board for colored plaid-patterned template

pencil and ruler

plumb line

lots of low-tack painter's tape

water-based glazing liquid

damp cloth

level

RECIPE

1 part latex paint

1 part water-based glazing liquid

note to mom or dad

Make a colored diagram of your plaid pattern before you start. To avoid paint leaking under the tape, press the tape down firmly and apply a thin coat of paint over and away from the tape.

For best results, prepare your surface following the instructions in the Start Right chapter, pages 14–27.

step 1　Apply 2 coats of white base coat and let dry for 4 hours.

step 2　On a piece of bristol board, make a colored template of the plaid to use as a reference.

step 3　(Shot 1) Using your plaid template as a guide, with ruler and plumb line, measure and mark off the vertical stripes on the walls. Place the tape along the outside of the spaces to be painted. Our large blue stripes are 9″, and the space between the large blue stripes is 21″. Thin blue stripes are 2″ and thin red and yellow stripes are 1″. Tape an X in the spaces that are not to be painted.

step 4   (*Shots 2 and 3*) Mix the colored glazes. Follow your color pattern and roll the blue glaze onto the corresponding wide and narrow vertical stripes.

step 5   (*Shot 4*) Roll the red and yellow glazes onto the corresponding narrow vertical stripes. Remove the tape carefully by pulling it back on itself. Wipe any leaks with a damp cloth. Let the glaze dry completely. The drying time varies with the type of glazing liquid used. As there is so much taping involved, it's best to wait overnight.

step 6   (*Shot 5*) Using your plaid template and the level, measure and tape off the horizontal stripes. They are the same as the vertical stripes.

step 7   (*Shot 7*) Roll on the colored glazes as you did vertically. Carefully remove the tape and let dry.

theme
rooms

One of the easiest ways to choose a design for a children's room is to work around a theme. It could be a favorite sport, a trip to the beach, or a beloved cartoon character.

slam dunk

My friend Anthony designed this basketball court for his son's bedroom floor. The floor was already varnished when he started the project. He began by drawing out a basketball key in proportion to the size of the room. The area was taped off and then sanded lightly to remove some of the sheen of the existing varnish. A high-adhesion primer was then used to create a tough grip between the floor and the base coat. Two coats of latex paint in bright NBA colors were used, and once thoroughly dry, 5 coats of high-gloss varnish were applied. This well-used bedroom floor is an enormous success for both father and son.

nautical dreams

A beautiful old fireplace mantel made a quaint headboard for a little boy's bed. The width is the exact size for a single bed. It was first cleaned up and then primed and painted in 2 coats of fresh white paint. Nautical stencils were used to decorate the surround. It was secured to the wall and the narrow firebox opening stuffed with pillows.

by the beach

You do not have to live beside the beach to have a room with a seaside theme. Katherine loved her holiday cottage, so her mom created the atmosphere of sizzling summers in her daughter's city bedroom. A color palette of royal blue and white was painted on the walls, woodwork, radiator, and furniture. Existing paint on the sleigh bed's footboard was sanded down by hand. Then artist's acrylics were used to create a simple beach mural. Satin varnish was applied for protection.

flower power

Once upon a time there were two sisters, Jade and Dejah. They each had their own rooms, and they both loved flowers. Jade, who was eight, wanted hip flowers that would match her passion for pink, but her older sister leaned toward wild-flowers and meadows. Both girls spent endless hours plotting and planning and sketch-ing out their ideas on paper. In Jade's room we opted for stenciled daisies (see Daisy Floor, page 58, for instructions) and amazing painted cardboard furniture (see Resources, page 174). Dejah's love for the outdoors and horses was brought inside by creating a mural of trees, grasses, wildflowers, and insects. We also made a headboard to look like a gate. The girls were thrilled with their rooms and incredibly proud of their work.

pretty pillowcase

Thin art-and-craft foam can be cut and glued onto a pillowcase. These are in the shape of flowers. We also added decorative beads. This project and pillow are not safe for small children.

note to mom or dad
Babies and small children tend to bite off beads and buttons and could choke, so save this project until after the toddler stage.

cardboard fireplace and throne

Furniture made from cardboard is a fantastic idea for young children. It can be painted and decorated in any design, and is sturdy enough to be used by an adult.

MATERIALS AND TOOLS

cardboard furniture (see Resources)

white and pale blue latex paint, satin

2 foam rollers and paint trays

star stencil, many styles available at craft stores, or to make your own: cardboard, marker, X-acto knife

low-tack painter's tape

paper towel

step 1   *(Shot 1)* Apply 2 coats of white base coat.

step 2   *(Shot 2)* If making your own stencil, draw the design (we used an eight-point star) onto the cardboard and cut out with a sharp knife. Tape stencil in position. Apply pale blue paint to roller and roll off the excess onto a paper towel. Fill in the stencil.

step 3   Add any other decoration or accents. Let paint dry for 4 hours.

step 4   *(Shot 3)* Assemble the furniture according to the instructions.

step 5   *(Shot 4)* Touch up any crevices or missed spots with paint.

flowery ceiling light

Many rooms have these round ceiling lights, which are functional but not much fun in a child's room. We transformed Jade's into a giant daisy. Eight identical petals were cut out of sheets of white Con-Tact paper and pressed around the light.

magic
meadow

Dejah loves animals, especially her golden retriever, Rex, and horses. A magical meadow was the perfect theme for this little girl. The ceiling was painted in soft lavender, and the walls were painted in cream highlighted with an aqua border. This is a good solution if you have no moldings or trim. Dejah and I decorated the walls with stamped trees and flowers, but the grasses and cattails were created by cutting lengths of Con-Tact paper in three colors.

Flowers were first stamped along the bottom of the wall. Then Con-Tact paper was cut into long blades of grass. I used dark green, dark taupe, and beige. The darkest color goes on first, then the taupe, and finally the beige. This gives a realistic depth to the meadow. I finished off by adding one or two stripes of dark green and cattail heads to the tops of some of the stems and stamping on butterflies and bugs.

fanciful trees

In keeping with our outdoor theme, simple trees were stamped onto the walls. I first painted the trunk by running the edge of a sponge roller up the wall to the height of the leaves. I then took a large piece of upholstery foam and cut it into a wavy cloud shape. I adhered a piece of foam core cut in the same shape to the back for support so that I could stamp an even impression. A thick layer of paint was rolled onto the foam side and then pressed against the wall.

MATERIALS AND TOOLS

low-tack painter's tape

pencil and ruler

chalk line (optional)

level

dark brown latex paint, satin

foam corner roller or 2″ paintbrush

indelible marker

upholstery foam, approximately 1″ thick

scissors or utility knife

foam core

white craft glue

leaf green latex paint, satin

water-based glazing liquid

mixing container

roller and paint tray

step 1 Mark out on the wall where the trees should go using low-tack tape.

step 2 Use a pencil and ruler (or chalk line, if preferred) to mark in the tree trunk. Check that it is straight with a level. Fill in the trunk by applying the brown paint vertically using the edge of a corner roller, or fill in the tree trunk by hand.

step 3 Draw out a naive treetop onto the upholstery foam with the indelible marker and cut it out.

step 4 Trace the treetop onto the foam core and cut it out. Glue the foam core to the foam.

step 5 Mix the green glaze and pour it into a paint tray. Use a roller to apply the glaze to the foam.

RECIPE

1 part latex paint

3 parts water-based glazing liquid

step 6 (*Shot 1*) Press the foam stamp into position on the wall. Press down evenly over the entire surface, and lift off the stamp without smudging the paint.

step 7 (*Shot 2*) While the glaze is still wet, make swirls randomly over the treetop with your finger to create the look of leaves.

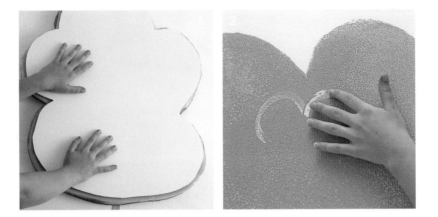

gate headboard

MATERIALS AND TOOLS

green-brown and white latex paint, satin

water-based glazing liquid

mixing container

3″ and 2″ paintbrushes

soft, clean, lint-free rags

RECIPE

1 part latex paint

2 parts water-based glazing liquid

A headboard was made for a single bed from 1″ × 4″ pine rubbed over in grassy green paint with a wash of white to give the illusion of a faded farmhouse gate.

step 1 (*Shot 1*) Mix the green-brown glaze. Use the 3″ paintbrush to apply the glaze to the wood; then wipe off the excess with a rag to reveal the wood's grain.

step 2 (*Shot 2*) Dip the 2″ brush into the white paint. Remove the excess onto a rag and dry-brush over the top of the wood to give it an antiqued quality.

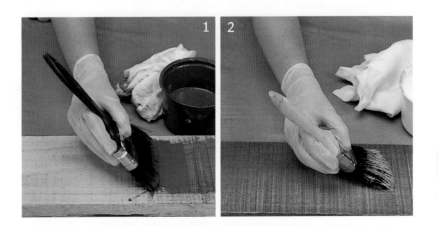

snow- boarding snug

Snowboarding has become a cult sport, even a lifestyle for many young people. Specialty stores are filled with clothing, accessories, stickers, and posters, as well as the actual boards. My sons live to "hit the slopes," so when I designed Max's bedroom it was easy to come up with a theme that would appeal to him. The walls were painted in bright colors inspired by the Hudson Bay blanket. The most interesting part of the bedroom was an alcove with the bed tucked in. Here we created a mural with photo images of Max snowboarding. In the summer both my sons switch to skateboarding. We used some old worn-out boards as shelving.

skateboard shelves

Used skateboards are battered and often split, but their interesting shape makes fabulous shelving. If you don't have any, you can find old boards at yard sales that cost next to nothing. If the colorful art or decals have rubbed off, add some new ones with paint or buy logos at sport stores. Here I removed the wheels from the bottom of each skateboard and then gave the boards a good scrub. I love the battered worn designs on the bottom, so I left as much of the existing pattern as possible. They were attached to the wall with metal brackets, painted the same bright orange as the walls.

snowboard montage

MATERIALS AND TOOLS

dark blue and white latex paint, satin

rollers and paint trays

measuring tape

a roll of wide freezer paper (available at specialty paper stores or your local butcher)

scissors

black marker

spray adhesive

low-tack painter's tape (optional)

color photocopies of snowboarder in action (8″ × 10″)

color photocopies of craggy rocks (various sizes)

wallpaper paste

1½″ foam brush

satin acrylic varnish and foam brush (optional)

I took pictures of Max snowboarding; he actually just posed on his board in different positions. The film was put onto a compact disc (CD) and then I printed out the pictures on a printer. The alcove was first painted a deep navy blue and then freezer paper was torn into a length of jagged mountains. This was laid over the top third of the wall, and a coat of white paint was rollered over the other two-thirds. When the paper was removed it gives the silhouette of mountains. I made fifteen photocopies of a picture of jagged rocks and snow and stuck them along mountains in an irregular pattern. The snowboarding pictures were cut out, leaving a little of the blue sky bordering the figure. This surreal picture is surrounding the alcove and makes a special place to hang out.

For best results, prepare your surface following the instructions in the Start Right chapter, pages 14–27.

step 1   Apply 2 coats of dark blue base coat and let dry for 4 hours or overnight.

step 2   Measure the width of the wall and cut a length of freezer paper to fit. Draw a craggy mountain range with a marker along the dull side of the freezer paper.

step 3   Tear the paper along the marked mountain range line.

step 4   Spray adhesive onto the shiny side of the top piece of paper and place the straight edge on the wall approximately 6″ down from the ceiling. Tape along the top if necessary.

step 5   (Shot 1) Apply a coat of white paint over the wall surface below and up to the paper on the wall. Allow a little blue to show through; this adds texture to the wall and makes it look more mountainous. To avoid leakage under the paper, roll a thin coat of paint on from the paper down onto the wall. Remove the paper and let dry for 4 hours.

step 6   (Shot 2) Take pictures of the person you want to be snowboarding; then have the film transferred to a CD. Print the pictures out on a color printer using good-quality paper. If you do not have a computer or color printer, any of these steps can be done through your photo developer and local photocopy outlet.

note to mom or dad

If you want the wall to be washable, add a few coats of acrylic varnish over the paper.

step 7   For the craggy rocks, make color photocopies of mountain ranges found in sports or climbing magazines. Use a variety of sizes. Cut the forms out.

step 8   (Shot 3) Draw a craggy range line 12–18″ underneath the mountain range. Use a little spray adhesive on the back of the cutouts of craggy rocks and stick them on along the line until you are satisfied with the design. Then use wallpaper paste and the foam brush to secure them permanently. Let dry.

step 9   Cut around all the snowboard photocopies, leaving about a ½″ border.

step 10 (Shot 4) Using wallpaper paste, adhere the snowboarders in various spots across the wall. They should move from high to low across the mountain range as if this was a real figure snowboarding down the mountain.

cool study space

The translucent colors and textures of water, ice, and snow were the inspiration behind a young lady's study area. Her main concern was to have a large work surface, so we took a hollow-core door and painted it to replicate the color and sheen of a huge block of ice. It sits on sturdy saw-horse legs bought from a lumber store. Their rough wood texture was disguised by painting them with metallic paint. We dressed up a cylinder-shaped lampshade with a couple of white feather boas, which have a hip and magical quality as they softly diffuse the light and sway gently if there is movement in the room. Wide vertical stripes of pearl and gray painted on the wall complete this beautiful but practical work space.

This lampshade is purely decorative, but its gentle quality is soothing after long evenings studying. Feather boas can be found in craft stores in many colors, but it is the delicate white ones that produce the softly diffuse light.

MATERIALS AND TOOLS

cylindrical lampshade
double-sided sticky tape
permanent spray adhesive
2 feather boas

step 1   (*Shot 1*) Remove the paper from one side of the sticky tape and stick a strip around the bottom and top of the shade.

step 2   (*Shot 2*) Spray the entire outside surface of the shade with the permanent adhesive.

step 3   (*Shot 3*) Start at the bottom, remove the paper from the tape, and stick the boa first to the bottom tape and then move up and around the shade. Attach the second boa where the first ends. Remove the paper from the top tape and finish by wrapping the boa around the tape. Clip off any excess.

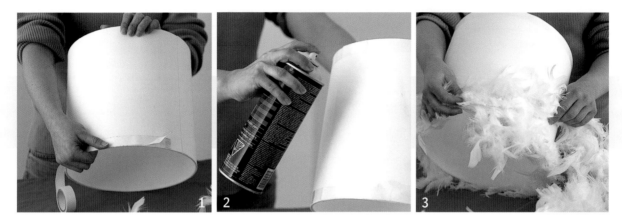

shag is back

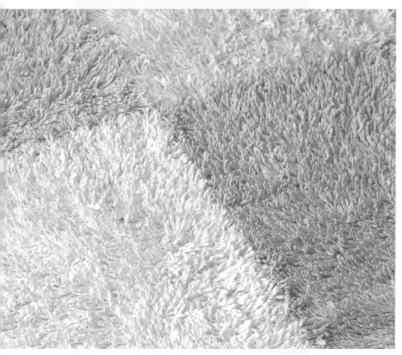

I have always loved the feel of knotted bath mats between bare toes. There seemed no reason to limit them to the bathroom, so we sewed six together with a heavy darning needle and string. The colors alternate between white and cream for a cool cozy rug that is also non-slip. To make it easier to sew, tape the pile down flat around the edges and then put wrong sides together and stitch. When the tape is removed, the stitches are hidden.

icy desktop

The problem with many children's desks that are available for purchase is that they are too small to hold a computer and printer as well as books and school notes. Your best option is to make one. You can buy either a tabletop made out of raw wood or a flat-faced, hollow-core door. The trestle legs we used here are available at hardware stores. They're rough wood but looked fine painted.

MATERIALS AND TOOLS

flat-faced, hollow-core door or MDF cut
   to size (ours is 32" × 48")

primer

aqua blue and pale aqua blue latex
   paint, satin

roller and paint tray

water-based glazing liquid

mixing container

craft paper

small amount of dark aqua latex or
   artist's acrylic paint

artist's brush

epoxy varnish (see Resources)

plastic spatula

gloss

or

acrylic varnish, fine-grade sandpaper,
   and foam brush

RECIPE

1 part latex paint

5 parts water-based glazing liquid

note to mom or dad

The paint-and-paper part of this project is great fun to do with the kids, but epoxy varnish is toxic; wear a safety mask and work in a ventilated area away from children and pets.

step 1   (Shot 1) Prime and apply 2 coats of aqua base coat to the top surface and edges of the table. Wait 4 hours between coats.

step 2   (Shot 2) Mix a colored glaze with the pale aqua paint. Roll the glaze onto the top and edges of the table.

step 3   (Shot 3) Cut a large piece of craft paper big enough to cover the entire surface of the table. Scrunch up the paper and then open it up and lay it flat onto the tabletop and around the edges. Smooth it lightly with an open hand.

step 4 (*Shot 4*) Lift off the paper. This will replicate the marks found in a block of ice.

step 5 (*Shot 5*) For the darker edges found in a block of ice, use an artist's brush and the dark aqua to draw a line around the top edge. Let surface dry overnight.

step 6 Apply the epoxy according to the directions in the kit. Smooth it over the tabletop with a plastic spatula or paint stick. Epoxy is self-leveling; that is, it fills all irregularities in the surface top to form a smooth level surface in a single application. It gives the illusion of many coats of varnish.

alternate method

If you are using varnish instead of the epoxy top coat, apply 5 coats, letting each coat dry before adding the next and sanding lightly between coats.

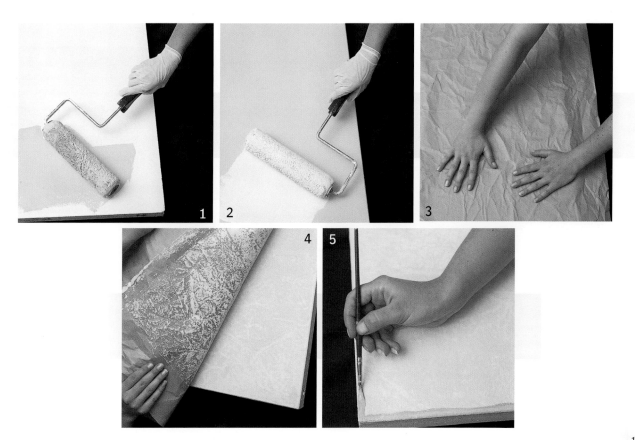

a fairy tale

When you're a five-year-old girl, princesses and castles are your own special world. Can you imagine the thrill of having your bedroom magically turned into the grandest of palaces? All you need is a fairy wand waved over plain walls to turn them into a shimmering golden yellow, decorated with glorious paneling and a ceiling that opens up to the heavens. And every princess must have a glittering crown, like this one swathed in fine fabric and precious baubles. A room as grand as this must have opulent lighting. The candelabras are made from cardboard, but once painted you would never know. This royal chamber makes an enticing place to invite your best friends for an afternoon of dress-up.

candelabras

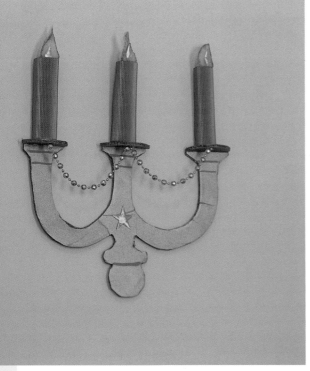

Although these grand sets of candelabras could be mistaken for the finest gold, they are actually just cardboard cutouts. The three dimensional effect is created by sticking on corrugated cardboard tubes cut to size. They are finished with small pieces cut into the shape of flames. With a little red paint added and some decorative gold chain, the illusion is breathtaking!

grand paneling

*plywood and skill saw or
    heavy craft paper and scissors*

pencil

ruler

level

low-tack painter's tape (optional)

white and fuchsia latex paint, satin

two 1″ paintbrushes

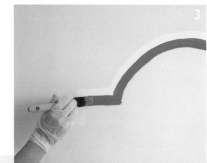

Fantasy paneling is easy to paint. Once the base coat is thoroughly dry, mark out large rectangles on the wall. They should all be the same height, but the widths can vary. I cut a template so that the rounded detailing at the top of the panels would match. I used white to paint a one-inch band around the panel. This can be done freehand or with tape. To create the illusion that the panels are recessed, I added a shadow line below and to the left of each white stripe. Usually I would use a darker tone of the yellow wall color, but for pure fantasy I chose fuchsia pink.

step 1   Decide where you want your panels to go, and what size they will be. Ours are 40″ wide. Draw and cut a template in the shape of the top of the panel. We used plywood, but heavy craft paper is fine also.

step 2   (*Shot 1*) Hold the template in position and trace around it with pencil. Use a level to make sure it is straight. Remove the template and draw in the rest of the panel lines with a ruler and pencil.

step 3   (*Shot 2*) Paint freehand over the pencil lines with a 1″ paintbrush and the white paint. (Use low-tack painter's tape as a guide if you wish.)

step 4   (*Shot 3*) Paint the fuchsia shadow line underneath and to the left of the white line, using a 1″ paintbrush.

royal bed

MATERIALS AND TOOLS

½" plywood

pencil and ruler

skill saw

plaster of Paris

newspaper

large pail

*yellow gold and antique gold paint,
    latex or acrylic*

3" paintbrush

foamcore

black marker

utility knife

hot glue gun and glue sticks

decorating accessories

sheer netting fabric

Every royal bed has a crown sitting majestically above it. First mark the wall where the crown is going to sit. It should be centered above the bed. Cut a piece of plywood to size. This will be the base of the crown. When the crown is attached to the wall, you will see only the underside, so this is the area we decorated.

step 1   *(Shot 1)* Cut out a piece of plywood in the shape of a stop sign cut in half. Ours is the width of the twin bed.

step 2   Mix the plaster of Paris with water following the directions on the package. Soak full pieces of newspaper in the mixture. Lay the paper onto one side of the plywood, making creases that look like fabric folds. Let dry overnight.

step 3   Paint a yellow gold base coat onto the dried newspaper. Use the antique gold paint and dry brush to highlight the folds.

step 4   *(Shot 2)* With the black marker, draw the shape of the top of the crown onto foamcore in sections to correspond with the edges of the plywood. Cut out the shapes with a utility knife. Paint these antique gold.

step 5   *(Shot 3)* With the decorated side of the plywood facing down, and using the hot glue gun, glue the foamcore to the edges of the plywood with a 1½" overhang.

step 6   *(Shot 4)* Attach gold balls, edge molding painted antique gold, and chains with the hot glue gun. Attach the netting to the inside of the overhang. Mount on the wall using L-brackets attached to the top of the plywood.

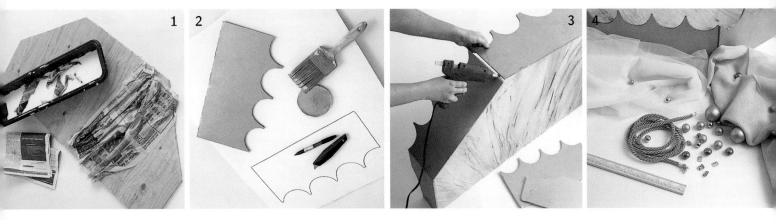

king of
the castle

Matthew had grown out of his baby crib, but this little chap is only two, so we devised a brilliant way of utilizing a standard bunk bed that would see him through the next ten years. Once assembled, these wooden beds are designed so the bed can be raised higher and higher off the floor as the child matures. When he is over six years old he can sleep on the top bunk and a lower one can be added for sleepovers, or the space underneath used as a desk area. But for now Matthew is still too small, so the frame of the bunk bed is used to form his own castle, inside of which he can play or sleep. We painted panels of canvas to resemble the stone castle walls. Windows were cut out and doors painted on. Each panel was then attached to the frame of the bed with Velcro strips. A sheet of Masonite was cut into turrets and painted to match the canvas walls, then nailed onto the top of the frame. When Matthew is old enough to sleep on the top bunk (the height can be adjusted) he will be able to look over his castle walls. When he grows out of his castle games, the canvas and Masonite can be removed and the bed can be returned to its original purpose.

We also took tall, thin melamine cupboards and attached cut pieces of Masonite to the doors. They were painted in the same way as the castle. Matthew now has two spaces for all his toys that are camouflaged within the castle walls.

castle bed

medium weight canvas

measuring tape

pencil

white glue

metal ruler

scissors

primer

pale, medium and dark yellow, off white, medium and dark wood brown latex paint, satin

roller and 3 paint trays

kitchen sponge

1/2" artist's brush

2" or 3" paintbrush

masonite

jigsaw

medium grade sand paper

velcro

Large pieces of canvas were cut to surround the bunk bed. There are two pieces for the front of the castle, and each can be folded back and secured to the Masonite posts with Velcro when the king is ready to get into bed. I used a sponge and three shades of yellow paint to create the mottled colors found in stone. Then I painted the wooden door and windows with a brush and added dark brown lines to represent the shadows between the wooden planks.

step 1   Measure and cut the canvas to size. Turn under any unfinished ends 1/2" and glue down with white glue. Prime the canvas and apply 2 coats of medium yellow paint with a roller. Let dry overnight.

step 2   (Shot 1) With ruler and pencil, divide the canvas up into 6" × 12" blocks. Draw in the windows and door where appropriate.

step 3   Pour the dark yellow and pale yellow paints into separate paint trays. Dampen the sponge with water and wring it out. Dip the sponge into the dark yellow paint and rub the paint into the rectangular blocks roughly, staying within the lines. The areas need not be fully covered with paint.

step 4   (Shot 2) Dip the same sponge into the pale yellow and rub randomly over the top of the dark yellow to blend and shade the blocks. Vary the color in each block as you would see in real stone.

step 5   (Shot 3) Dip the artist's brush into the off-white paint and create grout lines by painting over the pencil marks. Round off the corners for a more natural look.

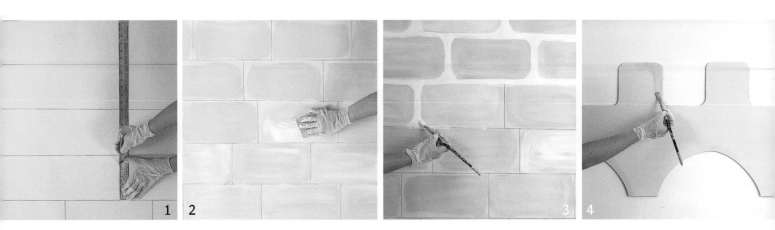

step 6   Use the 2″ paintbrush and medium brown paint to fill in the windows and door. Apply the paint in one direction, the same way the grain runs in wood planks. Use the artist's brush to apply the dark shadow lines between each plank.

step 7   (*Shot 4*) For the top of the castle, draw and cut out the turrets from the Masonite. Sand the edges. Apply primer and base coat as for the canvas. With the artist's brush, add dark yellow shadow lines and off-white highlights to give depth to the top and side edges of the turrets.

step 8   Hang the canvas pieces in place with Velcro.

wooded surprise

To make your own magical forest, all you will need is a large sona tube. These can be purchased at hardware stores and are traditionally used for concrete molds. They also make great trees! Mix up a bucket of paper mâché and then stick the soggy newspaper around the tube and mold the paper into the rough shapes that resemble the bark on a tree. Once dry, apply a couple of shades of brown paint. A piece of upholstery foam is cut into the shape of the foliage and painted green. Stick the foliage to the front of the tube with a hot glue gun. Plastic red apples are an added touch.

up the path

Floor mats are the most wonderful way to add color, pattern, and fantasy to a small child's space. When you are only two years old you spend most of your day playing on the floor. A floor mat can depict so many play themes, from roads (see Neighborhood Floorcloth pages 150–153), railways, oversized board games, or, for Matthew, his kingdom. Lakes, fields, and a pathway up to his castle were all painted on a piece of linoleum. Traditionally floorcloths are made from canvas that is stiffened once the paint dries but it never lies completely flat, not a good idea in a child's room. Linoleum sits firmly on the ground (no gluing in place is needed) and can be rolled up and taken with you if you move house. It is the paper-backed underside of the linoleum that is used, not the patterned side. It is first primed, then painted, and your theme is drawn over the top. Once the piece is finished, apply 2 coats of varnish for durability.

castle views

MATERIALS AND TOOLS

white latex paint, satin

roller and paint try

pencil

*pale blue, leaf green and bright
yellow latex paint, satin*

foam roller and tray

1½" paintbrush

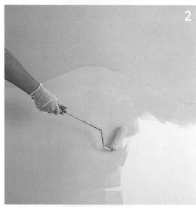

The walls were painted with rolling hills so Matthew can keep an eye on his kingdom. First a wavy pencil line was marked around the lower half of the room. Keep in mind the child's height when deciding on the horizon line. The walls were painted blue above the line and green below. A one-inch yellow line was painted along the top of the green hills and then blended with a slightly darker green. This highlights the top of the rolling hills just like sunshine and the darker green creates the illusion that the hills are rounded. Distant evergreen trees were painted on the wall with simple brush strokes.

step 1   Apply a white base coat to the walls and let dry for 4 hours.

step 2   (*Shot 1*) Draw a hilly landscape around the room with the pencil. The height should range from 2½ to 3½ feet. Apply 2 coats of pale blue paint to the walls above the pencil line. Let dry for 2 hours.

step 3   (*Shot 2*) Apply a coat of leaf green latex paint loosely below the line with a foam roller. Shade areas close to the bottom of the wall darker.

step 4   (*Shot 3*) Use the small paintbrush and yellow paint to cover the line of the landscape. Add dabs of yellow over the hills to create perspective. Blend with a bit of green.

talking curtains

Finger puppets add character to simple blue curtain panels. They are glued along the top in front of the clear plastic tabs.

playrooms &storage

If you are lucky enough to have a separate space in your home where children can play and keep their abundance of toys and games, it is usually in the basement. Families spend a great deal of time in these below-ground spaces that often have little natural light, wood paneled walls, and low ceilings. Why not cheer them up with interesting colors and turn them into imaginative great storage areas?

I'm often asked if you can paint over wood-paneled or wood-veneered walls, both of which are very common in North American basements. The answer is, yes you can. In fact, it's generally not a good idea to remove the paneling unless you are prepared for a large repair job on the walls. Paint is the next best solution, but the panels must be properly prepared for the paint to adhere. It's imperative to clean the surface first with TSP or a mixture of water and vinegar to remove grease and dirt. Then apply a coat of high-adhesion primer, which will adhere to the stain and varnish on the existing panel surface. Once the primer is on, a couple of coats of fresh water-based paint will produce an immediate transformation. You cannot disguise the indented lines on the wood, so instead incorporate them into your design by creating stripes; the added bonus is that the measuring is already done for you.

Whatever surface you are covering, choose colors that are bright and cheerful and will reflect the light. If you have a creative bent or are feeling adventuresome, try your hand at a mural. Use all the available tools to make the job easier, such as photocopiers, tracing, stenciling, stamping, and faux paint techniques. You will be dazzled by what you can accomplish.

Furnishings should be practical and comfortable with hard-wearing surfaces. Low games tables and brightly patterned floor pillows or bean bags are child friendly. Good overhead lighting is more efficient and safer than lamps—no cords to trip over. Install a dimmer for quieter times while watching TV or a movie.

Storage is one of the most important elements in a child's room. Children acquire stuff at an alarming rate, and unless it can be tucked away out of sight, their rooms will never look clean. Today there are plenty of affordable storage solutions. Transparent plastic boxes can be used for easy identification of clothing, toys, or art sup-

plies; baskets and bins come in a variety of sizes and materials including heavy cardboard, metal, wicker, or canvas.

Decorating and renovation stores sell unfinished furniture that is meant to be painted or stained in your own personal style. The advantage to these pieces is that they require no stripping or sanding. Once primed they can be painted simply with a child's favorite colors, and they can be stained, stenciled, or decoupaged in patterns to complement the room.

Secondhand furniture is easily transformed with all the same techniques. More preparation is required, however. The upside to this is that a dresser or storage trunk can be completely updated as your child grows from the baby years to preteen (see Preparing Furniture for Paint, page 24).

Look for ways to conceal the clutter. Inexpensive fabrics come in fabulous prints, or you can create your own patterns. Use Velcro or grommets to hang over shelves or replace a cupboard door. This makes easy and safer access for little fingers.

Make the most of every inch of your home for keeping everyday items at bay. Think "under" for children so they can tidy up themselves —under the stairs, under the bed, a row of baskets under a bench.

Although children will never admit it, life in an organized space is simpler. If you can add style and a touch of whimsy to the practical approach, all the better.

painted
panels
playroom

This basement playroom was drab and uninviting. It had pine paneled walls, a low ceiling, and a collection of mismatched furniture discarded from elsewhere in the house. It needed fresh colors and a spirit to match the exuberance of the children who play here. Once the walls were properly prepared, I applied lively mint green- and gray-colored glazes over a white base coat in alternate stripes. The tile ceiling was painted in a pattern of Neapolitan ice cream shades, visually fun for small children. The dark mismatched furniture was blended together by applying a white base coat and gray glaze to them all and adding new hardware. The results are a young and cheerful atmosphere, and this family now has a playroom everyone can enjoy.

before

Wood paneling and acoustical tile ceiling will do nothing to inspire play and imagination. A fresh coat of paint will do wonders to brighten up any paneled room.

painted wood paneling

Many recreation rooms and cottages have wood or veneer paneling on the walls. This common building material is inexpensive and may have been a quick solution to cover up unfinished or even damaged walls. If you are tired of the look, rather than pulling it all down, it is easy to brighten up the room by simply adding a coat of paint. Use the natural breaks and indentations in the panels to your advantage as a guideline for stenciling or, as we have done here, to demarcate a striped pattern.

MATERIALS AND TOOLS

wood filler

spatula

medium-grade sandpaper

*oil-based primer if wood is raw to seal
knots or high-adhesion primer if
there is paint or varnish on the
paneling*

*white, mint green, and pale gray latex
paint, satin*

roller and paint tray

water-based glazing liquid

2 mixing containers

container of water

3" stiff-bristled paintbrush

1" foam brush

soft, clean, lint-free rags

RECIPE

1 part latex paint

1 part water-based glazing liquid

note to mom or dad

*Use safety precautions when preparing
and priming the paneling, and keep
children and pets out of the room.*

step 1   (*Shot 1*) Fill in any holes with the wood filler. Let dry and sand smooth.

step 2   Prime the paneling. If you are using an oil-based primer, wear a mask and work in a well-ventilated space. If there are no windows, use a fan and take frequent breaks. Let dry overnight.

step 3   Apply 1 coat of white latex paint as a base coat and let dry 4 hours.

step 4   (*Shot 2*) Mix the mint green- and gray-colored glazes and sit them beside a container of water. Dip the stiff-bristled brush into the green glaze and then into the water. Apply the thinned-down paint to the wall, working from top to bottom in long straight lines, going back over your strokes where necessary to create a translucent strié effect. This paneling had thin grooves and I left every other thin groove unpainted.

step 5   (*Shot 3*) Fill in the unpainted thin grooves with the gray glaze and the foam brush. Make sure to get into the cracks and wipe off any excess with the rags.

colorful acoustic tile ceiling

This Neapolitan checkerboard makes a delightful change from the utilitarian acoustic tile ceiling. When painting over these tiles, always use latex paint and apply no more than 2 light coats. Otherwise the weight of the paint will distort the tiles and possibly pull them down. A primer isn't necessary unless you are covering up stains.

MATERIALS AND TOOLS

- low-tack painter's tape
- brown, pink, and mint green latex paint, satin
- 3 small foam rollers and paint trays
- water-based glazing liquid
- 2 mixing containers

RECIPE

- 1 part latex paint
- 1 part water-based glazing liquid

step 1   (Shot 1) If you are painting a checkerboard design, begin by taping off around every other ceiling tile.

step 2   (Shot 2) Fill in the tape-free squares with the brown paint. Remove the tape and let dry for 4 hours.

step 3   (Shot 3) Mix the pink glaze. Working on the white tiles, divide each tile on the diagonal and tape off the lower triangle. Roll the pink glaze onto these triangles. Remove the tape and let dry for 4 hours.

step 4   (Shot 4) Mix the green glaze. Tape off the upper triangles and roll the green glaze onto them. Remove the tape and let dry.

1   2   3   4

painted furniture

The fitted pine furniture was given the same treatment as the walls, but with just the gray paint over white. The original hardware was kept intact (see Preparing Furniture for Paint, page 24).

adventure
playroom

Although painting a mural can seem daunting, there are several ways to achieve this type of fantasy decor without having to be an artist. Pictures can be copied from children's books, and there are also many stencils available; but if you feel that you cannot manage this, why not employ local art students for the job? They will be glad for the work, and it should not be too expensive. Here a magical mural transforms all the walls into a kingdom of castles and dragons. The artwork was taken right over the top of the electrical box, the doors, and even the window blinds. The decoupage toy chest is a project that the children can take part in (see Bug Box, page 146).

the gang's headquarters

Hiding spaces have always been a favorite with small children, whether it's a cave made from sheets and chairs or a treehouse at the bottom of the garden. My children used to spend hours playing in the tiny cupboard under the stairs where we kept the vacuum cleaner. They painted this space to look like an army dugout. When I was asked to help two small future soldiers build their own army headquarters in a small space in their basement, I remembered the ideas and imagination of my own children. I painted a camouflage pattern on the ceiling and pasted old school maps on the walls. Maps can be found at school supply stores, but as the world's borders are constantly changing, you may be able to get some out-of-date ones from your school for free. I trimmed off all the unnecessary edging and cut the maps to size. I used several here and adhered them to the walls with wallpaper paste. Canvas tent flaps were attached to the front to keep the enemy out.

canvas zippered door

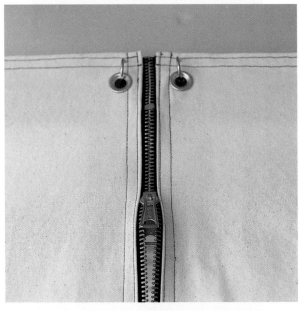

To hide Oliver from the bad guys and his parents, I made a tent flap from two pieces of strong canvas. A heavy-duty zipper was sewn onto the center edges, and grommets were inserted along the top edge to attach the canvas to a line of hooks on the wall. Grommets were also used halfway down both door flaps, and hooks were screwed into the wall so that the flaps could be held open when the enemy wasn't about. The finishing touch was to stencil on the letters *HQ* using fabric paint.

camouflage ceiling

To get a mental picture of the camouflage design, take a look at a piece of camouflage material. It's a mix of greens that swirl together as you would see in the jungle. There is no right or wrong pattern here; just use your imagination.

MATERIALS AND TOOLS

dark army green, gray-green, olive-green, blue-green latex paint, satin

roller and paint tray

pencil

2" paintbrushes

For best results, prepare your surface following the instructions in the Start Right chapter, pages 14–27.

step 1 Apply 2 coats of army green base coat on the ceiling and let dry for 4 hours.

step 2 (Shot 1) With the pencil, draw camouflage shapes over the surface. Mark which ones should have the different shades of green.

step 3 (Shots 2–4) Apply the gray-green, then the olive-green, and finally the blue-green paint. Let dry.

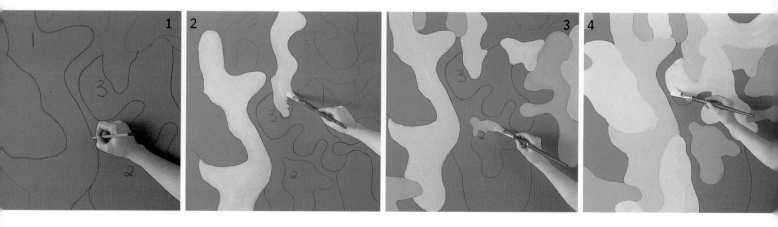

noogie land

I was honored to be asked to be involved in the decoration of a house being renovated into a "Gilda's Club." Gilda Radner, one of the world's funniest comediennes, died of ovarian cancer in 1989. Gilda's Clubs are welcoming places where anyone suffering from cancer can go and meet other people and share advice. Each place has an area where children who have cancer or who have a parent with the disease can be left to play while their mother or father spends time in other areas of Gilda's Club. These play areas are called Noogie Land. For this Gilda's Club in Montreal, we were given carte blanche with the design. First, I visited a kindergarten for decorating advice. I asked the children what would make them feel better if they were sick, and the consensus from these five-year-olds was bright colors, animals, and jungles. That became the theme of this playroom. The murals look complicated, but they were stenciled with a technique called projection stenciling. Any image can be projected onto a wall in any size. Projectors can be rented, or small handheld ones are available from craft stores. We took drawings and enlarged them to cover the whole wall surface. You can either draw your own pictures or use children's books. Freezer paper was used as the stencil paper; we cut it out with an X-acto knife and then stenciled it with latex paint and rollers. This method of stenciling enables anyone to be an artist. (For more on projection stenciling, see Resources, page 174.)

new wave of vinyl flooring

Vinyl flooring is once again popular, but the new designs and patterns available are far more interesting than the 1970s versions. Vinyl is immensely practical for children's rooms, as it is soft to walk on, nonallergenic, and easy to clean. A new process allows for photo images to be imprinted onto the surface of the vinyl, and the choices available are imaginative and great fun. There are many designs such as water, leaves, nuts and bolts, and, as we used here, grass.

kindergarten
madness

When my children were toddlers they loved to draw on the walls. I spent their first few years constantly scrubbing off marker, lipstick, and crayons. When I was asked to paint the walls for a family of preschoolers, I decided to work this penchant for wall art into the decor. A whimsical skyline silhouette was painted in green blackboard paint at child's height around the room. The children can spend endless hours decorating the walls with chalk. The challenge, of course, is to keep their artwork in the playroom! The blue walls and ceiling were covered in an assortment of floating bubbles painted with pearlescent paint, and the tiny basement window was hung with colored hoops that create a dancing pattern of reflective light across the room.

hopscotch carpet

Painting on carpet is a great way to revive tired wall-to-wall carpeting or stained areas. Draw your design first with chalk, as the paint is impossible to remove if you make a mistake. This popular hopscotch design makes a fun indoor game for the kids. Use latex paint or thinned-down artist's acrylics and a stiff long-bristled brush. Use a small but even amount of color and build up the desired depth. Brush the paint into the weave of the carpet so that it does not collect on the surface, as this will feel crusty to the touch. If this play carpet is going over a bare floor, I suggest you secure it to the floor with double-sided tape to stop it from slipping as the children hop about.

chalkboard mural

MATERIALS AND TOOLS

pencil
photos to copy
low-tack painter's tape (optional)
blackboard paint
1" and 2" paintbrushes

Look for photographs of skylines and rooftops to use as a guideline when drawing the outline. Windows, church spires, and smokestacks add a realistic touch, and a castle turret or two is great fuel for the imagination. Chalkboard paint is available in colors; here we used dark green. Look for it at craft stores.

note   If you are intimidated by the idea of drawing the skyline freehand, take photocopies of different skylines found in photographs or books, and blow them up to a realistic size for your mural. You can then use these to trace the skyline onto the wall.

For best results, prepare your surface following the instructions in the Start Right chapter, pages 14–27.

step 1   (*Shot 1*) Over a dry base coat, draw the mural outline. If you have a lot of windows to paint around, you can tape them off to speed up the process, but this isn't necessary.

step 2   (*Shot 2*) Fill in the mural, using a brush and the blackboard paint. Follow the manufacturer's guidelines for drying time required before using chalk on the surface.

stained-glass hoops

Tapestry hoops comprise two circles, one slightly smaller than the other, designed to hold fabric taut. Instead of fabric we have used pieces of colored acetate to make reflective windows of color that dance in the sunlight.

MATERIALS AND TOOLS

colored acetate, 1 sheet per bubble

safety scissors

tapestry hoops in different sizes
   (2 hoops make a set)

X-acto knife

transparent thread

screw-in hooks (1 for each hoop)

note to mom or dad

Supply your child with safety scissors for cutting the acetate, and do the final trimming yourself.

step 1   For each bubble, cut out 1 square from the acetate a few inches larger than the tapestry hoops.

step 2   (Shot 1) Separate the hoops, place the acetate square over the inside hoop and press the larger hoop over it. Tighten the tension with the screw until the acetate is flat and taut.

step 3   (Shot 2) Trim the excess acetate with the X-acto knife.

step 4   Tie different lengths of clear thread to the tapestry hoop screws and hang the colorful hoops from hooks screwed into the ceiling.

1   2

under the circus tent

There is no greater excitement for a child than a visit to the circus, so why not create your own tented playroom for your little ones? This room has a flat, low ceiling, but by painting wide blue stripes in a slight curve, they give the illusion that the ceiling is vaulted and high. The walls have been color-washed in sky blue above and blue and yellow below to resemble sky and grass. Simple valances were made from a small quantity of fabric with a fanciful children's design.

festive valance

This fabric valance fits directly over the windows that are fitted with painted wooden blinds. The valance is made 1 inch wider than the window opening and one-quarter of the window's length. Fabric padding was used to add stiffness to the fabric. Draw a symmetrical shaped pattern the size of the valance on a piece of paper. Add ½ inch all around for seam allowance. Use the pattern to cut two layers of fabric and one layer of fabric padding. Sew the pieces together, right sides facing, with the padding in the middle. We included red piping along the scalloped edges and up the sides for a decorative accent. Leave a foot open along the top for turning. Flip the valance right side out, hand-stitch the foot-long opening closed, and press. Add a strip of Velcro to the top and sides of the valance, and glue the corresponding strips to the wall.

tented ceiling

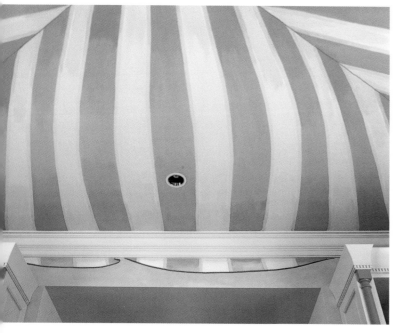

To be sure, the measuring for this wonderful trompe l'oeil tented ceiling is the biggest part of the project. But taken one step at a time, it is not difficult. You just need patience and frequent breaks for neck rubs. Study the photograph to see how the stripes curve about two-thirds of the way from the center of the ceiling to form the billowing effect. They also increase in width at the billowing point. The stripes are all hand-painted, starting with the bright yellow stripe that separates the blue and creamy yellow. The scalloped tent flaps that show underneath the molding are the final realistic touch, trimmed with painted orange/red cording.

MATERIALS AND TOOLS

chalk line

right-angle metal ruler

pencil

damp rag

creamy yellow, bright yellow, medium blue, and one shade darker blue, a small amount of dark gray and orange/red latex paint, satin

1/2" and fine artist's brushes

2" paintbrush

water-based glazing liquid

mixing container

matte acrylic varnish

varnish brush

or

sponge roller and paint tray

RECIPE

1 part latex paint

4 parts water-based glazing liquid

a little water

For best results, prepare your surface following the instructions in the Start Right chapter, pages 14–27.

step 1   (*Diagram 1*) Snap chalk lines corner to corner. (The stripes will meet at these lines.)

step 2   (*Diagram 2*) Using a ruler and pencil, draw faint lines cutting the 4 triangles in half.

step 3   (*Diagram 3*) Make pencil marks every 6" along the faint pencil lines.

step 4   (*Diagram 4*) There are now 8 sections. The stripe pattern in *A* will be the same as the other *A*, and *a* will mirror *a*. The stripe pattern in *B* will be the same as in the other *B*, and *b* will mirror *b*.

step 5 (*Diagram 5*) Draw in light perpendicular lines in one section *A* and one section *B*.

step 6 (*Diagram 6*) Make marks along the perpendicular lines as guidelines for drawing the stripes. To create the bulge, the stripes start thin, grow wider, and then thin out again. You want the bulge about two-thirds from the center point of the ceiling, so do your calculations accordingly. The first stripe will be 3″ and the rest 6″. (When all the triangles are filled in, the 3″ stripe will join up with the 3″ stripe beside it to make 6″.) Add or subtract ⅛″ as you mark along the perpendicular lines, except for the first stripe. For example, along the first perpendicular line you will mark 3¹⁄₁₆″, 6⅛″, 6⅛″, 6⅛″ to the end of the line; along the next line 3⅜″, 6¼″, 6¼″ to the end of the line; then 3¼″, 6½″, 6½″; then 3⅜″, 6¾″, 6¾″. Continue to increase until you have reached the widest part of your bulge, then decrease the measurements in the same manner.

step 7 (*Diagram 6*) Connect the marks to draw in the stripes. Draw in the other sections following the setup in step 4. Frequently come down the ladder and look at your progress. It's easier to assess from a distance. Remove any unwanted pencil marks with a damp rag. You have now drawn out all the stripes on the ceiling.

step 8 With a ½″ artist's brush, paint in the narrow bright yellow stripes freehand over the drawn lines.

step 9 With the 2″ paintbrush, fill in alternate stripes with the medium blue and creamy yellow paint.

step 10 Mix the glaze with the darker blue paint according to the recipe, adding water until the glaze is the consistency of heavy cream. To create shadowing on the blue stripes, apply the blue glaze to each end, tapering the color off with clear glaze in the middle. This shadowing will accent the bulge in the stripes.

step 11 Use the fine artist's brush to paint in a gray line along the original chalk lines (step 1) to highlight the seam where the stripes meet.

step 12 Continue the stripes below the ceiling molding in a scalloped shape, and paint in an orange/red cord or piping trim to finish the edges.

step 13 Let dry overnight, and apply a coat of matte varnish.

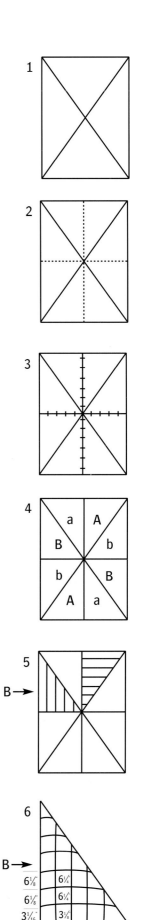

storage solutions

If you have space along a spare wall, or a corner that's not being used, these spots are perfect for creating an extra play area and some imaginative storage solutions. A long plank of wood or flat-faced door makes a wonderful work and play surface, with lots of room underneath for storage bins. Inexpensive shelving can easily be camouflaged with a youthful fabric drape. Repaint dressers to suit the age and personality of your young ones.

note to mom or dad
See Preparing Furniture for Paint (page 24).

arts and crafts table

This long worktable was designed for a household of tiny tots. The top sits on four wooden wall braces. An oversized cork notice board is a fantastic solution for the abundance of artwork.

patchwork dresser

This dresser started life as a raw piece of furniture. The plain pine was boring for a youngster, so I painted it in a pattern of bright cheerful colors and finished it off with brushed steel handles.

note to mom or dad

Metallic paint fumes are toxic when the paint is wet, so follow safety precautions and keep children and pets away. Metallic paint should not be used in a nursery.

battered metal dresser

A plain wooden dresser was transformed into a high-tech metal look for a teenager's bedroom. Metallic silver paint was applied over a coat of primer designed to adhere to the original varnish surface. The paint I used is Hammerite, which is available in spray and cans. Only a single coat is required for good coverage, but this paint is toxic when wet, so apply it in a well-ventilated space without the children present, and wear a mask. Once dry, this surface is extremely durable.

sky-high shelves

It can be tough for most kids to make the transformation from child to teen. They may be resistant to discarding their beloved toys, even though they are lacking space as the more grown-up furniture moves in. Here I built a shelf from planks and home-made wooden brackets that circles the room 18 inches from the ceiling. Painted in the same way as the Battered Metal Dresser (page 143), it gets all this boy's favorite things off the floor and out of his cup-boards, but he can still get comfort from his childhood memories.

functional filing

New filing cabinets can be purchased at hardware stores for very little money or can be picked up at yard sales and secondhand office supply stores. They make great bed-side tables with plenty of storage for books or midnight snacks. Metal cabinets need to be cleaned and sealed against rust with a metal primer. They can then be painted with either a water- or oil-based paint. Here I used high-gloss enamel paint in a vivid yellow but painted the fronts of the draw-ers with blackboard paint. The drawer pulls were left in their original state.

storage under wraps

A playroom can never have enough shelving or storage in the constant quest for keeping the jumble of toys off the floor. Standard, inexpensive wood shelving units are readily available. They are practical and rarely attractive, but they can easily be dressed up to hide the clutter and, even better, fit into a room's theme. Here sheets of tough canvas were decorated with stenciled words and attached to the front of a pair of freestanding shelves with Velcro.

bug box

This cut-and-paste project is one you could do with your children. Let them pick the theme and find cutouts to suit their fancy. A note of caution: Remove any locks or clasps from chests or trunks for the child's safety. This old trunk was so heavy that we removed the lid.

MATERIALS AND TOOLS

chest or toy box

acrylic primer

*white and pale green latex paint, matte
or satin*

water-based glazing liquid

mixing container

sea sponge

gift wrap or color photocopies of bugs

scissors

decoupage glue

1" foam brush

satin acrylic varnish

2" or 3" foam brush

RECIPE

1 part latex paint

1 part water-based glazing liquid

For best results, prepare your surface following the instructions in the Start Right chapter, pages 14–27.

step 1   Prime your chest and apply 2 coats of white base coat. Let dry for 4 hours.

step 2   (Shot 1) Mix the green glaze. Dampen the sponge with water and squeeze almost dry. Dip the damp sponge into the glaze and rub it over the chest to create a soft green mottled background for the bugs.

step 3   (Shot 2) Using scissors, cut out all the bugs.

step 4   (Shot 3) Place the bugs on the chest, moving them around until you are satisfied with the look. Then apply glue with a foam brush to the top and bottom of each bug and place it back in position. The glue goes on white and dries clear.

step 5   (Shot 4) Apply 3 coats of acrylic varnish to secure the paper bugs and protect the surface.

rainy day projects

When I was a little girl I dreaded miserable rainy days, stuck inside with nothing to do. I come from the north of England where it rains a lot! In those days we did not have computer games, e-mail, and chat rooms; nor did we have videos, and television programs were limited to the evening. Hard to imagine. Horrid weather days were spent helping Mom bake and fold laundry, but if we were lucky, she would get out the paints and pots of glue and we would sit around the kitchen table making or decorating projects. These rainy days spent playing with Mom were a sheer joy, and I have revisited my childhood many times with my own children. It makes no difference whether they are rambunctious young boys or teenaged girls—it's always time well spent.

I've included a selection of projects for various age groups and interests. Some can be accomplished by children on their own; others will need supervision in part or in whole. We are lucky to have so many materials and paint products that are environmentally friendly and far safer to use than their historic cousins. Always read the labels on any product you and your children are working with, and follow the safety precautions carefully. Toxic fumes can have a faster and more serious effect on a child.

neighborhood floorcloth

MATERIALS AND TOOLS

paper-backed linoleum

primer

creamy yellow latex paint, satin

small roller and paint tray

neighborhood map

pencil

ruler to help with drawing

artist's acrylics and/or latex paints in your choice of colors (we used gray, medium yellow, blue, light and dark green, black, and brick red)

small artist's brushes, different sizes

sea sponge

photographs of interesting buildings photocopied to size

tracing paper

carbon paper

alphabet stencil

black marker (optional)

satin acrylic varnish

foam brush or varnish brush

Your small children's neighborhood is their whole world. Their route to the park, the local shops, friends' homes, and visits to the library make up their first geographical boundaries. Why not transfer the map of your area onto a floorcloth that can give endless hours of fun and be educational as well? When the children grow up, or you change addresses, this floor art can be framed and hung in the den as a lasting memento.

Rather than the traditional canvas, we used the underside of a piece of paper-backed linoleum for our floorcloth. It's a good alternative as it will lie flat and the ends don't have to be finished. Five coats of clear acrylic varnish will make it very durable and easy to wipe clean.

note to mom or dad

Ask your child to point out his or her favorite houses and other neighborhood sites, and take photographs to place on the floorcloth.

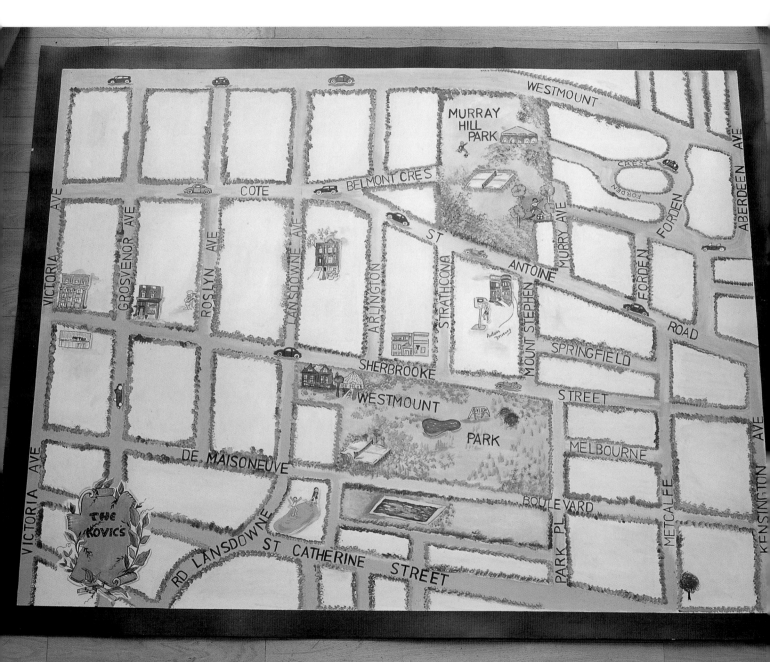

151

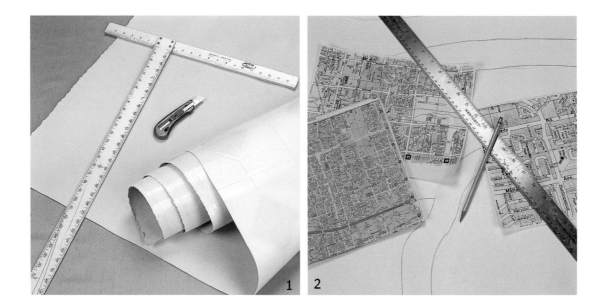

neighborhood floorcloth continued

step 1   (*Shot 1*) Work on the back side of the paper-backed linoleum cut to size. Prime the surface and let dry for 4 hours.

step 2   Apply 2 coats of creamy yellow base coat and let dry for 4 hours.

step 3   (*Shot 2*) Your city hall will supply you with a detailed aerial map of your neighborhood. Find your home and then decide on the size and scale of the area. You can cheat and make the recognized places more prominent and leave out the less-interesting areas.

3

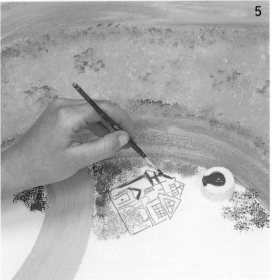

4

5

step 4   (*Shot 3*) Copy out a blown-up version of the map of your neighborhood onto the floorcloth with a pencil. Color in the streets with gray paint, the home lots with yellow paint, and the green spaces with green paint. Make little trees by dipping a small piece of sea sponge into darker green paint and dabbing along the streets.

step 5   (*Shot 4*) Buildings do not have to be in proper scale. Trace them from photos and use carbon paper to copy them onto the floorcloth.

step 6   (*Shot 5*) Color the buildings in with paint. Name the streets with the alphabet stencil or by hand using a marker, if you prefer. Add a few cars on the streets, a mailbox, a park bench, anything that gives your neighborhood character. Don't forget your house.

step 7   Protect your floorcloth with 5 coats of clear acrylic varnish.

framing with fur

Fake fur has become one of the hottest style items not just for clothing and accessories but also for home furnishings. It is readily available by the yard in an enormous variety of eclectic designs. Look for wild animal prints or sumptuous white shag. I chose bright colors to decorate frames made from simple cardboard, but you can cover just about any surface with fur.

MATERIALS AND TOOLS

thick cardboard or poster board

ruler and marker

scissors or sharp knife

faux fur fabric

marker

hot-glue gun and glue sticks

or

white craft glue

note to mom or dad

Young children may have trouble cutting the fur as they should not use sharp scissors or an X-acto knife and should not help with the hot glue gun. But craft glue is safe for them to use.

step 1　(Shot 1) Decide the size of frame you want and draw it out on the cardboard. Ours is 9″ × 12″. Draw a centerpiece and cut it out so that you have a cardboard frame.

step 2　(Shot 2) Place the faux fur fabric fur side down on a flat surface. Lay the cardboard frame on top of it and use a marker and ruler to draw lines 1″ from the outside perimeter of the frame. Also draw lines 1″ in from the inside perimeter of the frame. Cut out the faux fur along these lines.

step 3　(Shot 3) Glue the faux fur to the frame using the glue gun. Apply glue only to the cardboard surface. Fold over the excess fabric to the back of the frame and press it down. Make corner cuts in the fabric so that it will lie flat.

note　If working with young children, it is safer to use white craft glue as the glue gun does get hot.

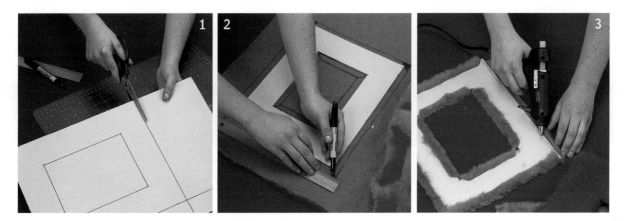

cd picture frame

stripes of molding or wood for frame

carpenter's glue

4 corner brackets

foam core

staple gun

burnt orange latex paint, satin

2" paintbrush

color copies of photographs to be framed

empty CD jackets (sold at office supply and music stores)

pencil

hot-glue gun and glue sticks

photos

note to mom or dad

Use caution when handling a hot-glue gun to avoid a nasty burn; the glue and gun barrel get very hot.

There are so many important occasions to capture as we grow up, and today photographs can be color-photocopied at a copy shop or printed off a home computer. Here's an interesting way to display photos of friends, pets, and parties. I mounted CD jackets, empty ones bought from an office supply store, onto a framed piece of foam core. The jackets open easily when the next group of photos arrives, and you don't have to take the display off the wall—just open the jackets and pop in the new pictures.

step 1   Have the lumberyard cut the molding to size. Mitered corners look more professional. Glue the corners together with carpenter's glue and secure with corner brackets.

step 2   (Shot 1) Cut the foam core a little larger than the inside perimeter of the frame. Using the staple gun, staple the foam core to the back of the frame.

step 3   Paint the front and back of the frame and the foam core.

step 4   Make color photocopies of your photos or print pictures straight from your computer. Cut them to fit inside the CD jackets and slip them in.

step 5   (Shot 2) Working on a flat surface, arrange the jackets on the framed foam core and mark the positions with a pencil. Use a hot-glue gun to secure them.

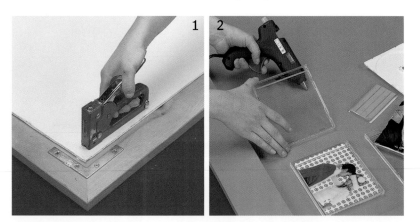

157

silhouette headboard

If you don't already have one, spend a sunny morning hunting through yard sales and you will always find old headboards. They can be restyled with paint to match your child's decor. Here we stenciled a silhouette of a city skyline that was copied from a post-card and enlarged on a photocopier. The silhouette was painted over an ombré sky. This is the natural effect seen at dusk as the day turns to night. It is easier to work on a flat-fronted headboard with little decoration or trim.

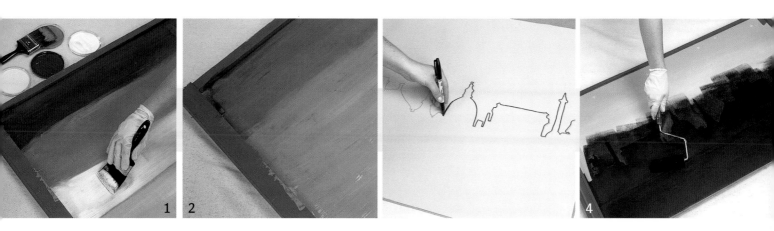

1 2 4

MATERIALS AND TOOLS

headboard, either new or previously painted

dark blue, medium blue, pale blue, white, and black latex paint, satin

four 2″ paintbrushes

soft, clean, lint-free rag

photocopy or drawing of skyline or chosen image

large sheet of Mylar or plastic

marker

cutting mat

X-acto knife

spray adhesive

small roller and paint tray

satin acrylic varnish

2″ foam brush

For best results, prepare your surface following the instructions in the Start Right chapter, pages 14–27.

step 1 Apply 1 coat of the palest blue base coat and let dry for 4 hours.

step 2 (*Shot 1*) Apply the darkest blue in a wide band along the top of the headboard. With a fresh brush, apply a band of the medium blue paint below this, allowing the top part to overlap slightly with the darker color. Next add a band of white, again overlapping the color above.

step 3 (*Shot 2*) While the paint is still wet, pull a dry brush through all the bands of color to blend them together. Let the headboard dry 4 hours or overnight.

step 4 (*Shot 3*) Photocopy or draw your picture to fit the headboard. Trace the picture onto a sheet of Mylar and then cut it out with an X-acto knife. The stencil will sit along the top of the headboard with the skyline cut out along the bottom of the Mylar.

step 5 (*Shot 4*) Spray the back of the stencil with adhesive and flatten it onto the top of the headboard. Apply black paint with a roller below the stencil cutout.

step 6 Carefully remove the stencil and let dry.

step 7 Apply 2 coats of varnish for sheen and protection.

splendid spongeware

Traditional spongeware has always been a popular choice for ceramic and tin kitchenware in country homes. You can create your own decorated mugs, plates, and jugs from standard white ceramics. Inexpensive white ceramics can be sponged with craft paint designed for this purpose and then baked in your oven to make the paint permanent. It will even be dishwasher proof.

Our hand-painted spongeware lines a shelf that has been trimmed with a streamer of paper butterflies.

MATERIALS AND TOOLS

plain white ceramic jug

pattern for sponging (we chose a
   butterfly)

tracing paper

pencil

carbon paper

Con-Tact paper

cutting mat

X-acto knife

low-tack painter's tape

blue ceramic paint

kitchen sponge

paper towel or newspaper

note to mom or dad

Kids love to sponge paint; make sure the sponge is almost dry.

step 1   (Shot 1) Either draw or trace the butterfly pattern onto a piece of Con-Tact paper or sticky-backed lining paper. Include a 1″ border around the design. Use a sharp knife to cut out the square and the butterfly design within the square. Cut out 2 or 3 design squares.

step 2   (Shot 2) Peel the protective backing off the butterflies and stick them onto the jug. Dip a small piece of sponge into the blue ceramic paint, dab the excess onto a paper towel, and then dab the paint over the jug, leaving some white showing. Let dry for 4 hours if you are going to stick Con-Tact paper over the painted surface to fill in the blue butterfly. Otherwise, let dry for 1 hour before putting in oven. Peel off the paper butterflies.

step 3   (Shot 3) To color in the white butterflies, peel the protective backing off the background squares and press into position over the white butterflies. Sponge paint this area in solid blue. Remove the background squares and let dry.

step 4   Bake in oven preheated to 300°F for approximately 40 minutes, depending on the brand of ceramic paint you use.

my magnets

MATERIALS AND TOOLS

    your chosen images, photocopied to size
    contact cement
    a sheet of plastic or acetate
    small rubber roller
    regular and safety scissors
    a strip of self-adhesive magnets
    spray varnish

note to mom or dad

Children can choose the pictures for their magnets and can cut out with safety scissors, but you handle the contact cement and the spray varnish.

Making personalized magnets for a bulletin board or refrigerator is lots of fun and every age can get involved. You'll need suitable images, which can be found anywhere from computer pop art to comic books, magazines, stickers, and decals found in variety and sports stores. You can even use family photos by photocopying your favorites in color or black and white, decreasing their size to about 1½ to 2 inches. You can buy self-adhesive magnets in strips and cut them to fit your project at most craft stores.

step 1   Apply the contact cement to the back of the image. If you are using many small images printed on one sheet, apply the adhesive to the whole piece. Stick the paper to a sheet of acetate the same size. Use the roller to press it down securely.

step 2   (Shot 1) Cut out your image neatly with scissors.

step 3   (Shot 2) Cut a piece of magnet to fit. Ours is about ½" square. Peel the paper backing off the magnet and stick it to the acetate back of the image.

step 4   Apply a coat of spray varnish to seal and protect the paper. (The image can bleed if brushed with wet varnish.)

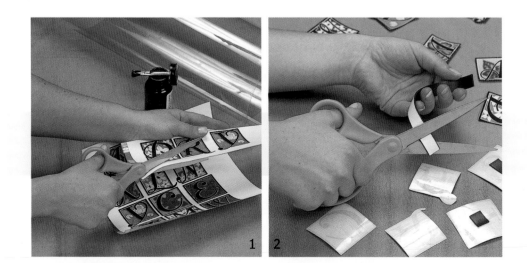

1   2

marble paper

The art of painting paper has been around for hundreds of years and is once again hugely popular, even though you can buy exotic printed papers. Marbleized papers have a magical quality and they are a delight to create with a child. They can be used for wrapping gift boxes, but these stunning pieces of art can also be framed. The technique is simple, but because artist's oil paints and paint thinner are used, young children should be most helpful making the gooey gel, not doing the actual painting.

MATERIALS AND TOOLS

saucepan

1½ cups cornstarch

cold water, about 5 cups

whisk

pan a little larger than the sheet of paper you are decorating (a plastic kitty litter pan works well)

artist's oil paints

paint thinner

artist's paint tray

¼″ or ½″ artist's brush

stir stick

paper with no plastic or wax in it from a paper or art supply store

clothes drying rack

iron

note to mom or dad

Oil paint is used here, which requires paint thinner to remove from fingers and brushes, so let the younger children help with the gel and laying the paper down, but not with the paint.

step 1 In a saucepan, dissolve 1½ cups cornstarch in 1½ cups cold water. Add 3 cups of water and bring to a boil on the stove, stirring or whisking constantly. Once boiling, take off the heat and pour into the large pan. Let it sit until it cools and turns to a thick gel, about 15 to 20 minutes.

step 2 (Shot 1) Mix artist's oil colors with paint thinner so that they are quite runny. Liberally apply the first color to an artist's brush. Then with a stir stick, tap and splatter the paint over the surface of the gel. Add as many paint colors as you want.

step 3 (Shot 2) Blend the colors slightly using the wooden end of the paintbrush, dragging it gently over the top and pulling the colors in different directions.

step 4 (Shot 3) Lay the paper flat over the surface, making sure that it is all touching the paint.

step 5 Lift the paper out carefully and carry it to the sink. Rinse the gel off the paper. It can be put right under the tap. The paint will adhere because it's oil.

step 6 Hang the paper to dry overnight. Using a low setting, iron the paper flat.

games table

Wooden supper tray tables can be given a dual purpose by transforming them into a games table. There are several ways to produce a checkerboard depending on how elaborate you want the results to be. For an elegant chess table, individual squares cut from two opposing colors of marble paper can be glued to the surface and then sealed and protected with several layers of varnish. For a simpler effect, I used a stencil and black and white paint.

MATERIALS AND TOOLS

wooden tray table, top surface larger than a checkerboard

medium-grade sandpaper

primer

small roller and paint tray

white and black latex paint, satin

checkerboard (for a template)

pencil

low-tack painter's tape

Mylar

ruler

marker

X-acto knife

cutting board

stencil adhesive

paper towels

gold paint pen

satin or semigloss acrylic varnish

2″ foam brush

step 1   Sand and prime the top surface of the wooden tray. Let dry for 2 to 4 hours. Apply 1 coat of white base coat and let dry for 4 hours.

step 2   Center the checkerboard on the tray top and draw around the perimeter with a pencil.

step 3   (Shot 1) Tape off around the inside of the square and apply black paint to the borders. Let dry for 4 hours.

step 4   To make the stencil place a piece of Mylar on top of the board. Measure and draw equal squares using a ruler and marker. There will be 64 squares.

step 5   Place the Mylar on a cutting board and cut out every other square on every other line. You should have 16 cutouts.

step 6   (Shot 2) Spray the back of the stencil with adhesive and stick it down in position on the white square, lining it up exactly. Dip the roller into the black paint, and wipe off the excess onto a paper towel. Fill in the cutouts, building up the color. A gradual buildup of color will prevent leakage under the stencil. Let dry for 4 hours.

step 7   Remove the stencil carefully. Make sure the back is clean. Reposition the stencil, moving over and down to complete the pattern. Fill in with black paint.

step 8   (Shot 3) Use a ruler and gold paint pen to outline the checkerboard.

step 9   Apply 3 coats of varnish for protection.

chinese lantern

MATERIALS AND TOOLS

1.5-liter plastic soda bottles

X-acto knife

decorative paper with Chinese motif

white craft glue

5 chopsticks

votive candle

glass container

note to mom or dad

Keep sharp scissors and X-acto knives away from young children. You cut the soda bottles and then let the kids decorate them. And never leave a burning candle unattended.

Summer barbecues call for innovative outdoor lighting ideas, and candles are always a favorite, but they do require protection from the breezes. These Chinese lanterns are not only easy and fun to make but will receive huge compliments from your guests. Most large cities have a Chinatown where you can find the most beautiful papers. If you don't have one near you, try a paper or craft store. These lanterns are designed to sit on a garden tabletop or alongside a wall. Note that the votive candles must be set into a glass container before you insert them into the lanterns.

step 1   (*Shot 1*) Wash out the soda bottles. Slice the bottoms and tops off with a sharp knife to create 12–13"-long cylinders.

step 2   (*Shot 2*) Cut the decorative paper to fit the cut plastic bottles. Run a bead of glue along the length of the cylinder and press one edge of the paper down along the glue line. Wrap or roll the paper around until it meets the first edge and glue in place, overlapping to form a ¼" seam.

step 3   Slide a pair of chopsticks onto the bottle and the paper for extra support and decoration. Place a votive candle in the glass container and set the container in the lantern.

monthly planner

This monthly chalkboard planner is a fun, decorative, and practical idea for children's busy lives. Cut a piece of Masonite to approximately 4 feet by 3 feet and apply a coat of primer. Once dry, apply 2 coats of blackboard paint. Using 2-inch molding, frame the painted Masonite. Lengths of ½-inch pine divide the surface up into days of the month. Once in place, secure with small nails. Wooden letters can be purchased from craft stores. The months and numbers are changed every four weeks but the days stay in place. The days were applied in different languages. These were painted then attached with nails in the appropriate places. Once the planner is hung, all that is left is to fill in the days with children's activities.

wine corkboard

You can either make or buy a flat-faced frame. This was painted in a strié of blue by pulling the paint across the raw frame. A solid dark blue line was painted ¾ inch around the outer and inner edge. Instead of applying a picture to the center, a checkerboard pattern of corks was glued inside the frame. Clean corks can be bought from winemaking stores. You may need to cut some of the corks to fit.

study wall

As children grow, so do their piles of paperwork. Grade-school kids seem to have more papers than their parents. Schedules for sports events, homework assignments, magazine cutouts, and notes from friends need to be displayed or they remain scrunched up in the bottom of schoolbags.

Bulletin boards can be easily purchased, but I find that they are never big enough for the typical family's clutter. There are several different materials that can be called into service to make your own. Here we have used a combination of blackboard paint, cork, and metal and covered an entire wall.

Chalkboard paint is now sold in a variety of different colors. I applied 2 coats of traditional black over a clean, dry wall with a low-pile roller.

note to mom or dad
Older children can help with the painting and cutting.

step 1   (*Shot 1*) Cork is available from art supply or craft stores by the roll, sheet, or as tiles. It is easily cut to size, but rather than gluing it to the wall (which is a nightmare to remove), it's better to glue it to a piece of plywood.

step 2   (*Shot 2*) I used simple wood trim to frame the corkboard, mitering the corners and attaching the trim with glue and finishing nails.

step 3   (*Shot 3*) Metal can be bought in sheets from hardware stores. It should be cut with metal cutters. The edges are very sharp so wear heavy-duty work gloves and sand down the cut edges with heavy-grade sandpaper. Attach the metal to the center of the corkboard with nails or screws, and frame as you did the corkboard to cover up the sharp edges.
Magnets are used to hold the notes to the metal. There's a wide variety available, or you can make your own (see My Magnets, page 162, for instructions on how to make personalized magnets).

Hang the bulletin board on the blackboard wall with strong picture hangers or plugs and screws.

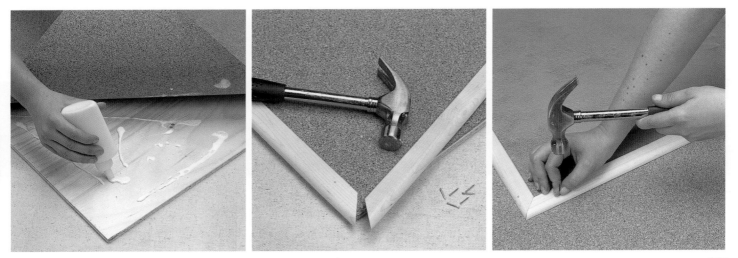

resources

Debbie Travis Specialty Collection

A line of specialty products such as glaze, suede paint, stone finish stucco and more for the contemporary, elegant interior. Available through the Painted House website, www.painted-house.com, or by calling 1-800-932-3446 (Canada & the United States).

Lynne Charest (p. 30)

Charest Associates Interiors
2155 Leanne Boulevard, Suite #208
Mississauga, Ontario
L5K 2K8 Canada
phone: 905-403-9388
fax: 905-403-9448
e-mail: Charest@interlog.com

primary colors

Designer's guild

Fabrics and accessories for the home.
267 Kings Road
London SW3 5EN
phone: +44-0-20-7243-7300
fax: +44-0-20-7243-7320
www.designersguild.com
info@designersguild.com

Heather Gilmour Herbert (p. 42)

Room by Room Design
20 Bermondsey Road
Toronto, Ontario
M4B 1Z5 Canada
phone: 416-285-1642
fax: 416-285-9553
heather_gh@hotmail.com

good knight

Torlys

Leaders in specialty flooring.
Head Office:
6155 Kestrel Rd.
Mississauga, Ontario
L5T 1Y8 Canada
phone: 905-612-8772
toll free: 800-461-2573
fax: 905-612-9049
www.torlys.com
postmaster@torlys.com

BioShield Paints

Environmentally safe, natural paints.
United States Sales: Michael Schwab
phone: 800-621-2591
fax: 505-438-0199
International Sales; Rudolf Reitz
phone: +1-505-438-3448
fax: +1-505-438-0199
www.bioshieldpaint.com
edesignco@aol.com

cute to cool

Epoxy Varnish

There are various brands available at home renovation centers or specialty paint stores.

Montreal Decorators

251 Ste-Catherine East
Montreal, Quebec
H2X 1L5 Canada
1-800-215-6910

purple haze

Colorworks by Jessica

Design painting kit.
725 Second Avenue North
Minneapolis, MN 55405
phone: 612-377-3910
fax: 612-377-2734
www.colorworksbyjessica.com
jmaurer317@aol.com

under the rainbow

Martin & Associates

Specialty products, stencils.
139 Labrosse
Pointe Claire, Quebec
H9R 1A3 Canada
phone: 514-697-3000
fax: 514-697-4116

flower power

Mixed Nuts

Cardboard furniture.
221 Rayon Drive
Old Hickory, TN 37138
phone: 615-847-8399
fax: 615-847-1167
www.crazycardboard.com
info@kraftables.com

noogie land

Projection Stencilling

An instructive book by Linda Buckingham and Leslie Bird. Hartley & Marks Publishers, Inc., Vancouver, BC, 1999.

LSI North America

Nature's floors perfectly replicated in grass encapsulated in durable vinyl.
200 West Beaver Creek,
Unit Eleven
Richmond Hill, Ontario
L4B 1B4 Canada
phone: 1-800-449-3916
fax: 905-731-8194
LsiTile@aol.com

kindergarten madness

Blackboard paint

This paint is now widely available in oil-based and water-based versions at your local home renovation center, paint store, or art supply store.

Low-tack masking tape should always be used.

To order:
Tape Specialties
615 Bowes Road
Concord, Ontario
M5A 2P3 Canada
phone: 1-800-463-8273
fax: 905-669-2330
www.thegreentape.com
tape.specialties@sympatico.ca

index